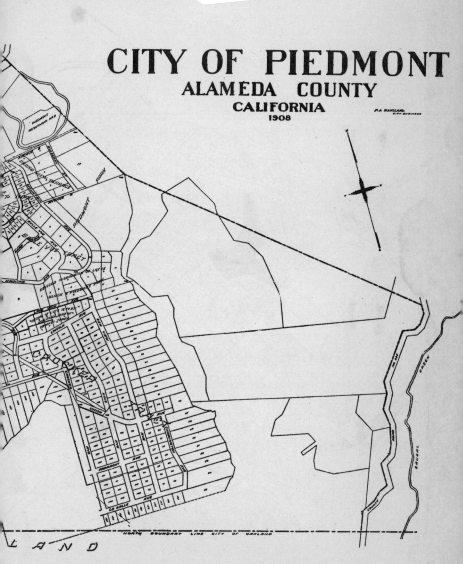

CITY OF PIEDMONT
ALAMEDA COUNTY
CALIFORNIA
1908

Queen of the Hills

Piedmont Park

Queen of the Hills

THE STORY OF PIEDMONT
A CALIFORNIA CITY

by

EVELYN CRAIG PATTIANI

THE ACADEMY LIBRARY GUILD

Fresno, California

1954

Lithographed By
SIERRA PRINTING & LITHOGRAPH CO.
Fresno, California

This book is lovingly dedicated
to the memory of my father
HUGH CRAIG

FOREWORD

For years residents of Piedmont and others interested in Piedmont have been wishing for some way of finding out about the earlier history of this small City and its surrounding country. Finally there has come, from the one probably best qualified by birth, residence and careful research, the excellent and meticulously exact history contained in the following pages. Mrs. Pattiani, the author, was brought up in Piedmont, her father was its Mayor, and in addition she is a careful and studious investigator into historical matters. The results of her knowledge, investigation and research are set forth in the following pages.

Allen L. Chickering.

INTRODUCTION

The word "piedmonte" has its derivative in Latin, meaning "foot of the mountain". Resting upon the slopes of Liguria, in northern Italy, is a peaceful city named Piedmont, that has long been famous for its homes and gardens, picturesque views and mild climate. Just how a California location acquired a title that is so appropriate to its own picturesque beauty is difficult to determine at present.

In the early 1850's many pioneers wended their way over the trails left by their predecessors, the Spaniards and Mexicans who had rancherias throughout this portion of Alameda County. In their search for fertile farmland, some of these pioneers may have envisioned a similarity of these hillsides to the terrain of a faraway homeland known in verse as the Piedmonte of the poets, in Italy, and thus bestowed the loved name upon this scene.

Beautiful Setting ...

There on the eastern shores of San Francisco Bay were green fields above sloping oak-dotted lowlands reaching out to the mountain peaks beyond. Through the rolling hills and ravines flowed sparkling sun-flecked streams, shadowed in their sheltered bends by buckeye and alder bushes. With such a romantic setting, it is fitting that an unusual city should have grown and flourished upon these hillsides facing the Golden Gate, through which one may watch the evening glow of sunset fade over the vast waters of the Pacific.

The basic idea of formulating such a sparsely settled community into a municipality began to gain force in 1900 and is almost without precedent. Those few who cherished the visions of such a city as the Piedmont of today, with its homes and terraced gardens, its schools, church and self-government, accomplished the first step of their objective in January, 1907.

Surrounded by Oakland ...

At the date of incorporation Piedmont had a very irregular borderline, and it was soon surrounded but certainly not enveloped by Metropolitan Oakland. The original dominating personalities have left an imprint for all time on civic affairs and in the governing body of its volunteer officials. We owe a debt to those who have built well for the future to present a record of their achievements.

In writing of this small but significant locality, I have of necessity interspersed the historical data with personal experiences and observations of my own. Perhaps these might be headed under "source material", for they are otherwise unrecorded. Quotations and statistics are given with careful adherence to the truth in every detail.

As an active participant in the changing scene through many years, I have endeavored to retain through research and memory the color and spirit in each succeeding period as they unfold before me.

Just as man, with his aspirations, dreams and fears, forms a background for the history of his own period, so this story is woven about the people who have played their part along the river of time flowing over the sun-lit hills of Piedmont.

Evelyn Craig Pattiani

CONTENTS

Walter Blair Home and Fields—1860s

EARLY PERIOD—1820-1850

The Name California...

The Piedmonte of our narrative is located within the confines of a state which owes its own name to a fanciful fairy-tale written long before America itself was discovered. California as a word has its origin in fable, but what the name means or from whence it was first derived remains an unsolved mystery.

Caliafia, so the story goes, was the name of an island far, far away where dwelt dark skinned people with a lovely Queen Calafia as their ruler. On this island, of course, was much wealth, including gold, diamonds, pearls and so forth. Thus it has been suggested that the early Spanish *conquistadores* optimistically coined from this word the name of California and gave it to the new land they were exploring north of Mexico along the Pacific coast.

Royal Land Grants...

The King of Spain granted through his viceroys in New Spain some 45,000 acres of what is now Alameda and Contra Costa counties to one of his soldier-explorers, Sergeant Don Peralta. This grant was dated June 3, 1820, under the regime of Pablo Vicente de Soto, the last of the Spanish governors of Alta California.

The entire historic background of the East Bay centers within the holdings of this grantee. Don Luis Peralta held his grant, Rancho San Antonio, intact until 1842. At this time he assigned to his four sons tracts of land extending eastward from the Bay.

To Jose Domingo he gave the northwest quarter and to Vincente the next adjoining portion, including *Encinal del Temescal,* then an oak grove where the Peralta home was located. The section of the domain later to be known as Piedmont occupied a site partly within both these portions, although the larger fraction of Vincente Domingo's became the present city of Oakland.

Climate Conducive to Farming...

The mild climate, abundant rains and fertile, virgin soil made it comparatively easy for the rancheros within the territory to keep their herds of cattle in pastures. The horses, too, were numerous and bred from famous stock.

As for entertainment the residents had their gay fiestas, fandangoes, rodeos and gory bullfights. The Spanish dons with their ladies thought nothing of travelling great distances, either on horseback or in carriages, to the various *haciendas* where colorful and lavish festivities prevailed.

Besides the keeping of livestock, the Spaniards found the soil especially well suited to the production of grain. And the trails carved out by the Peraltas in their rides between ranches are the thoroughfares of today.

Breaking up of the Grant ...

Gradually these Spanish grantees, still secure in their princely possessions, warily observed the growing number of settlers and "squatters" arriving in make-shift boats from the peninsula across the Bay. Many of these new-comers were traders who had made the trip with other mercantile groups from New England on the slow, tedious journey around the southern tip of South America, Cape Horn, and then back up to the harbor of San Francisco. Some of the adventurers remained, seizing homesites on the eastern shore of the Bay, and exchanged manufactured goods, which were greatly in demand, for the various local products, such as tallow and hides.

Thus the Peraltas often surrendered a parcel of their great store of land in lieu of the purchase price of a bill of goods or in order to pay some other debt. Because of this gradual eating away of the original grant, new small ranches were constantly springing up. The extensive holdings of this family, like so many other Spanish grantees, passed out of the hands of the original holders and their descendants.

Before leaving this period, it must be added that during the entire Mexican rule there were persistent efforts made to get the beautiful lands of California under some type of government control. Although these efforts were aimed particularly at the Missions, surrounded by their large holdings of lush lands, the government also eyed such estates as the Peraltas jealously.

Development of San Francisco ...

It is difficult to describe the growth of one particular section of the Bay area isolated from the larger and more important communities. From these neighboring cities have come to Piedmont a continuous tide of men and families, whose names and achievements are interwoven with the pattern of development of the Bay region as a whole.

By 1844 the government of the United States became increasingly aware of the westward trend of the people and abruptly awakened to the problems that were arising. So in that year a topographical expedition was sent, under the leadership of Lieut. John Charles Fremont, to explore the Pacific wilderness. This mission required Fremont to find the best route for the immigrant parties, which were constantly making the arduous trek across the plains and mountains down into the Sacramento Valley and Sutter's Fort.

Later explorations brought Lieut. Fremont to the Bay region and the town, then known as Yerba Buena. This name belongs to the aromatic vine (1) that grew profusely in the area. The meaning of the phrase *yerba buena* is "herb of healing", and the pungent aroma could be detected in almost any protected place: under wild blackberry bushes or hazel-nut trees, below the shiny leaves of poison oak vines, or wherever the virgin growth remained. It was native to the East Bay region as well.

However, the rapidly growing city changed its title to San Francisco in 1847, in honor of its Mission dedicated nearly a century before to St. Francis, through Maria Dolorosa.

California Ceded to the Union . . .

It was through the concerted efforts of Fremont and others of a like determination of character that the final acquisition of California was made; it was ceded to the United States in 1848, after winning its freedom from the Mexican government.

John C. Hayes . . .

Though the name of John C. Hayes holds a colorful place in San Francisco annals, it is also found in the earliest records of the Piedmont story. Before culminating his active career in San Francisco, Colonel Hayes had noted the possibilities of developing the mainland side of the Bay and had approached the Peraltas for the purchase of a townsite. With some other associates he bought up "all the dry land north of San Antonio Creek and west of San Antonio slough, and speedily developed the area into homesites for the settlers".

Colonel Hayes selected for his own use an extensive wooded portion in the hills immediately behind the present Piedmont. He constructed a wagon road leading to this property, widening the trail

(1) *California Historical Quarterly,* XXVIII, March, 1949, p. 23.

along the creek at the bottom of the ravine. This road was called Jack Hayes Canyon Road, but has since been changed to Moraga Road. Here at the intersection of the present Thornhill Drive he erected the family home, which later became famous for its collection of art treasures. A sister of Hayes married his great friend and business associate, Major R. P. Hammond, and their son became the engineer, John Hayes Hammond, of South African gold mine fame.

Naming of the Golden Gate . . .

To his home Colonel Hayes would often bring his friend, John Fremont, and from the heights the two men frequently watched the setting sun descend in golden glory into the waters of the Pacific. This sight inspired Fremont to give to the narrow straits the name of the Golden Gate:

Approaching from the sea, the coast presents a bold outline. On the south the bordering mountains come down in a narrow edge of broken hills, terminating in a precipitious point, against which the sea breaks heavily. On the northern side the mountain presents a bold promontory, rising within a few miles to a height of two or three thousand feet. Between these points is the strait, about one mile broad in the narrowest part and five miles long from the sea to the bay. To this gate I gave the name of Chrysopylae, or Golden Gate, for the same reason that the harbor of Constantinople was called Chrysoceras, meaning Golden Horn . . .

These men visualized a passageway through which the gold of Asiatic commerce would flow, enriching the whole of the United States.

SECOND PERIOD—1850-1870

Subdivision of Large Grants . . .

With the waning of the Peralta regime, the original land grants were gradually being subdivided and sold in smaller segments to the new settlers who were constantly pouring into California by way of the Isthmus of Panama, around the Cape of South America or by the weary land trek across the continent in covered wagons. These newcomers would ply across the Bay in rowboats from the San Francisco side to rudely improvised landings on the mudflats bordering the eastern shoreline.

On one such water-logged craft Walter Blair with his brother William took passage over to the sprawling village of Oakland and toiled up the trails leading to the foothills. These brothers had been reared on a Vermont farm and had journeyed to the western coast during that wild "rush" of 1850-1851. After considerable investigation about the land around the Bay region, they realized with true Vermont perspicacity the value of these fertile slopes rising above the oak-dotted plain beneath.

Blairs Establish a Farm ...

Records prove that in 1852, or thereabouts, Walter Blair purchased from the United States Government a tract of land consisting of 600 acres for the ludicrous price of $1.25 per acre. The boundary-line of this acreage extended from what is now the Mountain View Cemetery on the north, with Moraga Road as far as Scenic Avenue on the eastern side, then westward as far down as the Pleasant Valley Road, thence to the present Piedmont Avenue, and northward again connecting with the line later fenced in by the Cemetery Association.

The brothers selected for their immediate use a level campsite a short distance south of Hayes Canyon (Moraga) Road on a pathway which they called Vernal Avenue, but since has been changed to Highland Avenue. Here they discovered a clear spring of cool drinking water which trickled out from its rocky fount. They could see that an easily dug surface well would give an excellent supply for their cattle with much left over for the watering of their prospective garden. Walter and William set quickly to work building a one-room house, after choosing the site for it, and commenced a farming venture in the best New England tradition.

Upon this extensive ranch Walter planted his fields of wheat and barley and soon managed to purchase from his neighbors a stock of fine breed cattle. He built the barns to house these cattle on the east side of the dirt road which he had so appropriately called Vernal, because of the abundance of green fern and bushes growing along the way. Blair proved himself an aggressive and observing pioneer, and his ability and sagacity were to be valuable in the future development of this district in Piedmont.

Increasing Fame of the Dairy ...

With these herds of young stock feeding upon the grass that grew so easily from that fertile soil, the renown of the rich milk produced from them quickly spread from the local settlers out to the city across the Bay. With this popularity the demand for milk products steadily increased, and soon a spanking team of horses, dragging a heavy wagon, hauled the ten-gallon milk cans filled to the brim down through the dust or mud (depending upon the weather) of the streets of Oakland to the foot of Broadway daily. Here the teams were transferred to a creek barge which steamed its way to the opposite shoreline of San Francisco. After this brief respite the horses had to climb the steep cobblestoned streets to the homes of the wealthy atop Rincon and Nob Hills, whose demands made the trip necessary.

Not only did Blair popularize the Piedmont dairy industry, but his genial manner and personal friendship with many of these erstwhile customers induced them to visit the celebrated milk ranch. The guests, after inspecting the industry, were usually taken to the simple cabin on Vernal Avenue, where a bachelor's hospitality was dispensed.

Blair Alert for New Opportunities ...

Although the main business on this ranch was the supplying of milk and butter to near-by communities, the owner was constantly on the alert for the development of new ventures when the demand grew apparent. The thick dust on the trails during summer and the heavy mud and deep ruts of winter retarded the speed of the milk wagons and inconvenienced visitors. A hard surface road was needed. For this purpose a part of the rocky hillside, just west of and below the present Dracina Avenue, was blasted. It is known as Blair's Quarry and has produced a hard basalt rock very desirable for city streets.

After several years of working this quarry, however, it had to be abandoned, for the excavation filled with water to a depth of over thirty feet. It was discovered to have a centrifugal suction, making it dangerous for the boys lured there by the tempting appearance of the swimming pool. So many drownings occurred that it had to be closed for public use and is now guarded by the fences of the Piedmont Park Department Nursery.

First Car-Line in Piedmont ...

Apparently it was during the early sixties that the idea of a horse-car line shaped itself in the minds of Walter Blair and Samuel Howe, the latter a man of considerable means who had also come from New England originally. Putting their plans into action, the two men started a gang of workers laying the tracks for the proposed line beginning at Seventh Street and extending out Broadway to where that artery divided into another road running northeasterly as far as the newly

First Piedmont Hotel—1876

established Mountain View Cemetery entrance. On earlier maps this road was called Webster Street, but as it was widened and improved, it became popularly known as Piedmont Avenue, a name which continued on up into the terrain above it. How this title came to be given to that particular portion of Alameda County is merely conjecture. It seems to have appeared simultaneously with the formation of a land company of the same title. The officers of this company were close associates of Blair and Howe, and their undertakings were aimed at the coordination of the various projects.

Rediscovery of the Piedmont Sulphur Springs . . .

In a profoundly hush-hush atmosphere the news was released in the early summer of 1869 (1) of real estate opportunities and speculation for this profitable investment of capital in the foothills of Oakland centering around some live springs in a deep canyon two miles northeast of the heart of Oakland. According to information found in the Bancroft Library at the University of California, the following events occurred which created quite a stir of interest in the upland farming area in the hills back of the city.

"A group of white sulphur springs was 'discovered' not long ago about two and one half miles from Oakland on the farm of Mr. Reed. As a matter of fact the springs were actually 'rediscovered', as they had been found and used for the cure of rheumatism by the late Mr. Holmes formerly a prominent member of Congress from South Carolina. Mr. Holmes, having found by experience the curative values of the water, took up his residence on this farm and finally purchased half of it. After his death the importance of the springs passed out of the minds of the few persons who had any knowledge of them.

"But not long ago (1869) a shrewd citizen of Oakland (name unknown), having an eye for attractive building locations, made an offer for the entire Reed farm and, while walking over it, discovered the old bathtub which Mr. Holmes had used in his self-treatment . . . The farmer related the incident about the former use of a spring down in the ravine nearby which had been thought by some to have valuable mineral properties. This casually described spring turned out, upon examination, to be several strong white sulphur springs within a few

(1) Edward T. Planer discovered the earliest historical record on this particular section of Piedmont, and it is quoted with his permission.

yards of each other. The largest threw out a good volume of water and left a light gray deposit in its course. The water smelled and tasted like that of the white sulphur springs near St. Helena in Napa County.

Erection of Hotel Proposed ...

"When these facts had become known, the adjoining farm also was purchased by this Oakland speculator, making a tract of eight hundred acres in all. About a dozen prominent businessmen of San Francisco at once became interested in the purchase, and, according to the well-guarded plans, the summer of 1870 should see the erection of a large, commodious hotel on a commanding site of not less than two hundred acres overlooking the cities of Oakland and San Francisco and the Bay for many miles in extent. According to those in the know, the location is unsurpassed for beauty, and it is only about one and one half miles from the head of Lake Peralta (Merritt) or two and a half miles from Oakland's local railroad station at Seventh and Broadway.

"It is also understood that it is the purpose of the new proprietors to develop the springs and secure every attraction of a first class watering place within sight of the city. They have given the locality the name of 'Piedmont'. It is further believed that land not needed for hotel purposes will be offered in large villa lots at some future date."

Widening Interest in Piedmont ...

During the late sixties and early seventies a few flashes of the gaiety of the social whirl were reflected on the East Bay side from the city on the sanddunes. In San Francisco the population and wealth were rapidly mounting, and men began to look toward the less populated town of Oakland for permanent homesites. Many of these prospective buyers had fine trotting horses with surries and came to the east side aboard one of the barges to the end of the mud flat landings. Moreover, it is probable that a group of men already acquainted with the Blair dairy products found their way out to his ranch and were thus introduced to this section of Oakland. In fact some became so interested that they decided to start a business venture of their own, yet in close cooperation with the Blair-Howe projects.

In 1868 the Piedmont Land and Water Company was organized with A. Bigelow as president, A. W. Bowman as secretary and treasurer, and L. A. Booth, James Gamble and Walter Blair as the directors. Because of the encouragement provided by these associates, Blair extended his car-line from the junction at Mather and Piedmont Avenues on up the winding grades, through his own grain fields, turning south to the Sulphur Springs' grounds which the new company had acquired along with other neighboring ranches and acreage tracts.

Having this seemingly failure-proof setting for their venture, the officers issued a series of bonds, selling them to people of San Francisco who were constantly seeking new investments for their accumulating profits. Thus the Piedmont Land Company became a more important factor in the subsequent development of this section than is generally recognized. Cash was made available for the erection of the hotel, having the Sulphur Springs as the added attraction.

Formation of the Mountain View Cemetery Association . . .

Before recounting the activities of the Piedmont Land Company, it is necessary first to revert to the opening of Piedmont Avenue, a district which provides a close and important link with the story of Piedmont. Early in 1864 the original Oakland cemetery was removed from Nineteenth Street to its present site. This valuable piece of property was then purchased from Rev. I. H. Brayton by a group of public-minded men. They had assembled on the evening of December 26, 1863, at the telegraph office in Oakland with the purpose of launching a non-profit service of vital importance to the community as a whole. It was in this manner that the Mountain View Cemetery Association was formed.

At this meeting twelve trustees were named with Dr. Merritt nominated as chairman of the association. The other members of the board were H. Tubbs, R. W. Heath, William Faulkner, S. Persey, J. S. Emery, J. E. Witcher, George E. Grant, A. M. Crane, J. A. Mayhew, S. E. Alden, Rev. S. T. Wells and Rev. I. H. Brayton. After a short time this two hundred acre tract was plotted by the noted New York landscape architect of the period, Frederick Law Olmsted. He had been invited to California at this time to survey Yosemite for the federal government.

The "Moss Tract" . . .

With the new Blair-Howe horse cars on the Avenue out to the cemetery gateway, the intervening lands grew in value for homesites.

However, several pioneers of the day had already moved out in this direction, the largest holding being that of J. Mora Moss. He had bought the triangular piece of land just south of Moss Avenue (now MacArthur Boulevard) with Broadway on the east. Here was built a handsome residence surrounded by a beautiful garden. This estate has since been acquired by the City of Oakland and is now used as a public park and playground.

Adjoining the Moss Tract on the south was another large home built by Colonel Joseph Moss Little, a godson of Mr. Moss. Col. Little had quite an exciting career, having served in the Union Army during the Civil War, participated in the Vigilante battle in San Francisco and started a lumber business in Oakland where he erected his home, "Littlebank", in 1869. During a Grand Army Parade, I remember, he presented a thrilling and romantic figure as he rode a prancing steed at the head. This memory is particularly vivid for me, since it was the first parade I had seen and we watched it from the family carriage at Moss and Piedmont Avenue.

Col. Little's wife became well-known as a vocal soloist for the First Choral Society of Oakland, and the tall gracious woman gave generously of her time and talent for the cultural development of the community. There were two daughters and three sons in the family, and the youngest son, Weare, has been the chief clerk of Piedmont's civic affairs, since its incorporation in 1907 as a city of the sixth class.

More People "Move Up" ...

Montgomery Howe, already mentioned as Blair's partner in the horse car venture, built a large house between Piedmont Avenue and Howe Street, a few hundred feet north of the present MacArthur Boulevard.

The construction of this car line was constantly attracting new settlers, and a group of southerners were the next to take up their residence in this newly opened area. Two pairs of brothers, George and Lindsey Prather and Charles H. and Henry Gorrill, built large square houses on adjoining lots. Of similar architectural design were the homes of a Mr. Minor of Louisville, Kentucky and Mr. Staples, who was an insurance manager in San Francisco. From among this group of neighbors two outstanding women have made generous contributions to the welfare of their community: Mrs. Harry East Miller and the late Mrs. Harrison Clay, both daughters of the Lindsey Prathers.

The motives which seemed to urge these people who had just lately arrived from the congested eastern cities was not only to assure themselves of a roof over their heads but, more important, to have spacious grounds surrounding their home, where they might let loose their creative ability in the beauty of their gardens. This need for the forestation of the barren hillsides and the local demand for shrubbery induced the Blairs to initiate yet another industry, and they established a plant and seed nursery. The site chosen for this new pursuit was on Piedmont Avenue between Mather and Cemetery Gate. This was where the single carline from Oakland terminated. But for the downward journey the horses were turned, not the cars.

Dapple Greys Used for Car-Line . . .

In front of the Howe home was the "switch" where the downgoing car might wait many minutes before it was passed by the other car, with its team of weary horses pulling a heavy load of passengers on the upgrade climb. It was at this point that, under the observant eye of Samuel Howe, fresh spans were put to the hauling, for their master took enormous pride in his handsome "dapple greys" which were always young and spirited. The Piedmont Avenue line aimed to make fast trips in order to make connections with the San Francisco trains at Seventh between Broadway and Washington Streets.

Growth of the Lower Districts of Piedmont . . .

What has been called the lower Piedmont or the Avenue District continued to invite men of means and vision to buy homesites in this acreage. In the late sixties Jonathan Hunt built a rambling home for his family under oaks of his estate. The Hunts were a cultured family from New England, and they did more than their share in the literary and musical life of that period. This property was later known as the Glen Echo Tract after its subdivision into smaller sections for new houses.

The remaining acreage, bordering the avenue on the east and north of the Hunt estate, was acquired by George W. Hume who, with his brother R. D. Hume, grew to prominence in the early success of the salmon canning industry. Mrs. George W. Hume, his young wife, established the first Piedmont school, the opening classes of which were held in the living room of her home.

The Highlands (Requa)—1876

Development of the Junction Section ...

By this time more settlers were moving out Piedmont Avenue, and the section called "the Junction" was quickly growing into prominence. This was the area adjoining the place where Moraga Road crossed the red rock drive, one block south of Cemetery Gate. As soon as this neighborhood had been opened, the swing doors of the old-time saloon had made their appearance on the northwest corner. It was an excellent location for an enterprise. The adjacent frontage towards the cemetery was purchased by William Blair, brother of Walter. Here he and his wife, Penelope, who had come out from Ohio to marry him, took over the nursery, which had been started as a general seed and plant store, and specialized in the growth of cypress and eucalyptus trees from seeds obtained from Australia. These young trees were used by the Blairs for the forestation of the bare hills, the lining of various roadways and the division of property lines.

Once this nursery was fairly established, the Blair brothers next wanted to extend the horse car line to connect at the Junction with the Howe system from Oakland. This would mean that the line should curve up through the waving fields of wheat to the level of Vernal Avenue at Moraga. From that point the team of horses could trot along to the terminus, which was located where the park now stands, next to the Piedmont City Hall.

Until this line was superseded by the cable line, the "driving master" of the system, the Danish Martin Miller, always kept his patrons alerted to the hourly schedule from seven in the morning until the last car for the day left the Springs at six-thirty at night. On the hard up-grade climb the taste of the blacksnake whip was given unsparingly to the team. But the return trip, with the watering trough and a feed-bag filled with barley in the offing, was made in record time by these well-trained trotters, and many were the shrieks and thrills as terrified passengers alternately clung to seats and hats while narrow curves were rounded against cool westerly breezes. However, with the exception of those comparatively rare occasions when the hind wheels took a leap off the tracks, the Junction was reached without mishap and on schedule, for the Howe car was not known to wait. It had its own time to make in meeting the broad gauge trains at Seventh Street. It was quite a trek to San Francisco in those days!

Water System Needed ...

Before the upper hills behind Oakland could be really opened wide to the wealthy businessmen seeking picturesque and permanent home-sites, the problem of securing an adequate and durable water system had to be solved. Heretofore, the creeks and surface wells had been the sole source of supply.

To fulfill this need came the brilliant and outstanding hydraulic engineer, Anthony Chabot. His career began when, as a sixteen-year-old farm boy, he left his home in Hyacinth, Canada, and came to California in the first gold rush fever of 1849. For the next ten years he was engaged in mining near Nevada City. His particular work was the digging of ditches to supply the mines with water. In about 1856 he came to San Francisco with the hope of finding some new outlet for his seemingly boundless energy and of using his recent experience in the furnishing of water for hydraulic mining. His inclination toward enterprises connected with water led him to associate with John Bensley and A. W. von Schmidt as they worked to devise an aqueduct system to bring the waters of Lobos Creek into San Francisco.

When this project was accomplished, he came over to Oakland and as one of the original incorporators, along with Henry Pierce, organized the Contra Costa County Water Company. With characteristic energy and determination Chabot commenced the task of planning the water supply of Oakland and the outlying districts. The aqueduct first led directly from Temescal Creek, but this proved to be rather uncertain. So in 1868 work was commenced on the dam which was to form the Lake Temescal Reservoirs, and was completed in the latter part of 1869. The system was known as the San Leandro water service and had been transferred from the California Water Company to the Contra Costa Water Company in 1876 at the price of $806,191.49.

Anthony Chabot, who had spent so many fruitful years of his life in working out engineering problems for water distribution to the East Bay communities, died in 1888. It is fitting that the name of this man who hastened the development of the region should become a familiar word, with Lake Chabot, the Chabot Observatory and the Chabot Home. The descendants of his brother, Remi Chabot, now live in Piedmont and Oakland and have become an integral part of the community life.

The Ghirardellis ...

Before leaving the sixties it may be interesting to mention a few more of the early settlers whose names are so familiar to Piedmont. Perhaps the most noted of these is that of Ghirardelli. To everyone, young and old, it is synonomous with chocolate, and all enjoy the various forms of the flavor extracted from cocoa beans at the massive red brick factory at North Point Street, in the Marina district of San Francisco.

A colorful career and enterprising genius has marked Domenico Ghirardelli as one out of the ordinary. Leaving his home in Rapallo, Italy, he came first to Lima, Peru, where he became acquainted with James Lick, a Pennsylvania piano-maker. Both these men were destined later to be closely identified with this Northern California region. When news of the Mother Lode gold strike reached Lima, Lick decided to try his fortune in California and encouraged his friend to follow. Soon he arrived with his wife and two children. Prosperity and adversity each had their day as the wheels of the chocolate business turned.

During the sixties the family which had now grown to six children lived in a palatial estate in Oakland's fashionable West End. But the story of the patriarch and founder of the well-advertised Ghirardelli Chocolate is interwoven with our story. Since the early days the Louis Ghirardelli daughters, Mesdames Chris Jorgensen and Charles Cushing. They with their children have generously contributed to the cultural and civic life.

More Pioneers . . .

Besides these recognized names, there are others who were tramping the dusty roads that were to become the wide asphalt highways of today. The Will W. Garthwaites came to Oakland in 1864 from San Francisco, where they had been early arrivals. The Garthwaite name has since become well-known in banking and civic improvement circles. My own grandparents, the Samuel Fleming Gilcrests, made the trip by covered wagon from Ohio to Oakland, arriving during August, 1864, and purchased a home at Second and Harrison Streets. (2) Mesdames Garthwaite and Gilcrest were among the original nine members of the local Baptist Church, established during the same year at Eighth and Clay Streets.

In those days the young city of Oakland divided itself into various social districts, and many of the names registered on Oakland lists have since switched their loyalty and residences to the hills in and about

(2) *First Directory of the City of Oakland*, 1869, p. 167.

Piedmont. (3) Probably some remember long Sunday drives in open carriages or phaetons up over red rock roads, sometimes in the wake of a sprinkling cart, or else preceding it and eating perforce the dry, parched dust, unless the driver could persuade laboring horses to out-run the slower teams ahead.

Furthermore, some of the young sons came for long tramps on Sat-urdays, walking little-known trails, equipped with lunch boxes and sling shots or, for the older and more fortunate ones, guns. In these hills they would stalk their prey of quail and other wild game. Allen L. Chickering, now a householder on Piedmont's Sierra Avenue was one of these ardent hunters and is now an expert on California wild flowers with specimens of many in his garden.

THIRD PERIOD—1870-1890

Building of the Piedmont Hotel . . .

Returning again to the history of Piedmont itself, the next step it took toward notoriety was once more through the joint actions of the land company and the Blair horse-car interests. The Directors had chosen a location directly opposite the present bank and shopping center with a frontage on Vernal Avenue. They commenced their am-bitious project by constructing a hostelry in the simple style of that period. Below the gardens of the proposed resort, on the south side, rambled a sparkling stream, and out of several crevices along the banks flowed the pink and white waters of the sulphur springs. About these springs many medicinal claims had been made, and several San Francisco families had already been lured across the Bay to try them out.

When it was finished, the hotel consisted of two floors with wide verandahs encircling each. To the south and east were a few separate cottages and a latticed summer house. The gateway to the present Piedmont Park stands about fifty feet to the west of what was politely known as the "ladies' entrance."

At the extreme of the building a pair of heavy oaken doors opened off the spacious verandah into the Grand Saloon with its huge mirror reflecting, among other things, the rows of glass tumblers ranged be-hind the long mahogany bar. Along the walls were placed the typical

---

(3) Cf. Appendix I. For names of those in social districts.

barrel-backed chairs, and between each could be espied the heavy brown spitoons of old-time barroom fame. The center of the room was occupied by the characteristic billiard table, and at one side a pot-bellied, over-sized coal-burner stove. This sanctum was reserved strictly for the male clientele of the hotel.

Across the Avenue where the Community Center is situated stood a long row of stables, maintained by the hotel. There an army of grooms cared for the picked group of thorough-breds, and soon the resort became famous for its horses. Horse-fanciers gathered there, and it was a common sight to watch sleek trotters and pacers, harnessed to their two-wheeled sulkies, racing over the newly rolled rock roads. Fred Whitney served as resident manager of this popular hostelry, and James Gamble, president of the local telegraph company, had connections made between the hostelry and the telegraph circuit constructed by the government, which joined the East Bay and Walnut Creek. Thus the Piedmont Hotel continued to attract attention through the eighties, and was served faithfully by the Blair line bringing a never-ending flow of visitors to its doors.

Booth Builds Hazelwood . . .

With Land Company developments during the seventies the Contra Costa Water Company had been encouraged to extend its pipelines up as far as the Springs Park along Vernal Avenue. At this time water pressure was insufficient to give supply to homes higher up the hillsides. With the hotel as a focal point several officers of the Land Company acquired choice sites near-by for prospective homes.

Among these early opportunitists was Lucius A. Booth, associated with the Big Four of railroad acclaim, and Arthur W. Bowman. According to the old records, these two appear as private holders of adjoining properties. Indeed, the Bowman tract still is indicated upon the local maps, covering the block reaching out below Vernal Avenue between the Blair fields and the Springs.

However, Booth and his wife came over from San Francisco and, using the Hotel as headquarters, finally settled upon a six acre location adjoining the southern boundary of the Springs grounds. Their first shelter was a rough cabin in a fern-covered ravine, and here they spent their free holidays and weekends. A spring of clear, cool water bubbled from under a ledge close by the cabin, and beneath this an excavation was dug in order to retain the precious liquid. This shady nook was known for a generation as "Booth's Spring" to neighbors and the "hired help" alike, who were often seen on their daily trips carrying a demijohn in each hand, particularly during the warm summer months when it was the only source of fresh, cold drinking water.

Soon the Booths discarded their temporary rough-hewn cabin for a more pretentious, permanent dwelling on a high knoll from which there was an awe-inspiring view of the Bay. In this two story home they lived for many years, until it was burned to the ground on a cold winter's night. They named the estate Hazelwood, because of the great abundance of that plant which flourished in this locale. (1)

The Blair and Gamble Interests ...

Another of this group of financiers, James Gamble, built a large and substantial home on the block bounded by Magnolia, Hillside, Vista and Bonita Avenues in about 1874. A graceful driveway circled around the central house and led out to the barns and into the rear yard where a miniature farm of horses, cows and pigs lived off the fat of the land. It created a happy setting for the growing children, Mary, James, Fannie and Frank, but soon the enticements of town life proved too strong, and in the early eighties the family once again moved back down into the more populous city below. Piedmont transportation was limited to horse-and-buggies, except for the hourly pick up of the Blair horse car line.

With his investments in the various enterprises at last showing a goodly profit, William Blair erected a permanent structure on or near the original cabin site. (2) Gardens were laid out in a formal pattern on the west side, and while these were coming into bloom, this thrifty and confirmed bachelor traveled up to Benicia and surprised his friends by bringing home a wife. But Phoebe Harvey Blair, an educated young woman, did not relish her enforced isolation, and after a year's experimentation the couple moved down into Oakland. At the corner of Fourteenth and Clay Streets William had built and now owned the Centennial Hotel. Here on property adjoining the City Hall the family took up their permanent residence, for the carline running west along Fourteenth Street to the Southern Pacific Depot was yet another Blair enterprise to be supervised. The two daughters,

---

(1) After the destructive fire the Ransom School was later built on this property.

(2) Information on the Blair Estate was obtained from interviews with Mrs. William Blair.

Lizzie (Mrs. Roberts) and Mabel (Mrs. Squires), were born here, but both were later sent to Eastern schools and then to Europe for their "finishing".

Arthur W. Bowman, already mentioned, moved his wife and two babies into the vacated Blair home, accompanied by a retinue of cook, nurses, coachman and gardeners. Soon four more little Bowmans were to make their appearance on the Piedmont stage.

Requa Glamour Radiates in Piedmont ...

A name that was destined to permeate these hillsides with a glamorous sheen for more than a generation was that of Isaac L. Requa, for the associates and friends of this family were numbered among the prominent personalities of the era. Mr. and Mrs. Requa and their small son Mark Lawrence, came to San Francisco from the bonanza town of Virginia City, Nevada. They established themselves in the new and magnificent Palace Hotel where they lived for several years, and their daughter Amy was born there.

It was while at this hotel that Requa met his old Comstock crony and fellow-'49er, Lucius Booth who, with his wife and two little daughters, already had his weekend cabin in the Piedmont hills. Not needing much inducement, the Requas soon accompanied Lucius and his wife across the Bay to see for themselves the beauties of their country place. The view over the lowlands looking west out through the distant Golden Gate was, and still is, superb. The Requas became so enamored with the possibilities of the landscape and the mildness of the climate that they immediately purchased a twenty-acre tract adjacent to the Booth property on its southern boundary. This piece of land possessed one of the most outstanding homesites in the entire East Bay.

Wealth Pours into San Francisco ...

Momentous events were taking form in San Francisco with wealth fairly rolling in from the Comstock Mines, and mansions were mushrooming atop high Nob Hill. Fair, Mackay, Flood, O'Brien and Crocker built among the first, while Huntington and Stanford came soon afterwards. Connected with these ambitious enterprises were the bankers and financiers, Ralston, Mills and Sharon, who tried to co-ordinate their allied activities in Nevada gold fields and San Francisco's Montgomery Street.

Naturally, San Francisco with her teeming port and high vantage

The Gamble Home—1878

points became a mecca for these worshippers of wealth, and they built their homes on the city's heights where they could watch the merchant ships and freighters passing in and out of the harbor, laden with necessities and luxuries.

Instead of remaining neighbors with their business associates, the Requas chose to build their residence in Piedmont. The mansion with its high cupola was nearly two years in the building and was named the Highlands. Painted a delicate shade of buttercup yellow, the house stood as an East Bay landmark and could be easily picked out from the decks of ferry boats crossing the Bay on a clear day. The architecture and size of the building are identical with that of the Governor's residence in Sacramento. (3)

Lawns and gardens surrounded the buildings which made up the completed estate, and an asphalt driveway curved from the pillared gate to the wide front staircase, then continued around to the side entrance under the *porte couchere*. For well over a decade the Requa family welcomed through these portals the many fine equipages and their occupants, who came as guests. These friends were often some of the most prominent people of the day.

More Wealth Attracted to Piedmont . . .

To the east of the Requa property the extensive rolling acreage was bought by Judge E. B. Crocker, of the Central Pacific Railroad Company. Despite the fact that he never built on it, his name has always been used as the designating title of the tract. Another railroad tycoon, A. N. Towne of the Southern Pacific, bought up the two acres on the corner of Hazel Lane and Highland Avenue.

This site was later acquired by Dr. August Liliencrantz, who built a three-story house on it, and soon had his grounds laid out in an artistic arrangement of flowers and shrubbery. He lived here with his wife and three children, Todd, Edith and Guy, for about ten years. The doctor kept a large stable of six to ten horses for his own private use. Those were the days when a lively stepping mare was the only means of rapid transportation between one patient and another. He always tried to obtain comparatively wild animals, because the more spirited they were the faster it was possible to cover the ground. A doctor's presence lent a more civilized and secure air to the sparsely settled

(3) The author has been informed from a reliable source that the architect of the Palace Hotel designed this Piedmont dwelling.

community, and as a young physician just commencing his practice he was kept busy in and about Oakland. Since then, he became recognized as one of the leading practitioners of this entire region.

"Hillside Health District" ...

With the Piedmont Land Company families improving their private estates, the Contra Costa Water Company was at last induced to extend its water pipes, but still no farther than Vernal Avenue. This made an abundance of water available to the large holdings below. These, which included the Blair ranches, the Piedmont Springs Hotel and the Requa estate, had until this time been dependent on the rather doubtful services of private surface wells, springs and various pumping devices.

When these first residences had been erected in the "hillside health district", as it was called, the open countryside afforded plenty of space for wild animals to roam, and owners had to keep a sharp eye on all barnyard fowls to keep them from being devoured by hungry wild animals. Mr. Requa once reported that a coyote came into the Booth's yard one evening and carried off a small dog, a pet of Mrs. Booth.

Era Commenced by the Requas ...

Time has shown that the stately and distinctive yellow mansion of the Requas was to herald an approaching era of pretentious country homes which blossomed forth in choice locations throughout the countryside. The old *haciendas* of the Spanish Dons were largely a mellow memory, but they seemed to enjoy a renaissance at the hands of successful American businessmen. Through two decades of local suburban growth there emanated from the Requa home a friendliness and hospitality which seemed to establish an atmosphere of stability and a pattern for gracious living for the rest of our community. Illumination for this huge mansion with its adjoining servants' quarters, stables and sprawling barn was supplied by a private gas machine on the grounds. As yet, the Oakland gas company had not extended its pipes out as far as these hills, and electric lights were still in the most experimental stages.

Another name, unconnected with the Piedmont Land Company, Russel W. Wing, shows on an early (1873) map of the region. He purchased a good-sized acreage well up on the Mountain Avenue trail. Built on a knoll fronting south, the new home had been carefully planned by Mr. Wing and his wife and was surrounded by large gardens and neatly gravelled driveways. On a higher portion of this estate a stream of fresh water gurgled from an underground spring out into a constant rivulet. Mr. Wing channeled this water into the reservoir he had made, and pressure was sufficient to supply the chief household needs from here.

Lighting Facilities . . .

Except for the private lighting system of the Requas, the rest of the neighboring families used kerosene oil lamps, tallow candles and numerous tin lanterns with wobbly glass shades above their oil-soaked wicks. These contraptions always were placed in strategic positions outside the house, such as close to the kitchen door in constant readiness for emergency night work about the place or perhaps to light some strollers on their way to the hotel saloon.

A further development was in the offing, as the first tiny "schoolhouse" was inaugurated. While the Bowmans were still occupying the Blair house on Vernal Avenue, they often had as a guest a young Mr. Worcester, who presided as minister at the Swedenborgian Church in San Francisco on Sundays. He was quite an authority on the tenets of this little-known religion, and the quiet solitude of these hills appealed to him. Mr. Bowman soon had a cottage built for him on land company property facing Vernal Avenue, at the corner where Oakland Avenue now cuts across. A schoolroom was included in the structure, and here Mr. Worcester taught the four Bowman children.

On the other side of the opening extending above this cottage ran a north and south trail, and on the further side of this a large, square house was constructed by Mrs. Bowman's sister and brother-in-law, the Wrights, and their three children, Allen, Bertha and Alice. This newest homestead occupied the block on the northeast corner of the present Blair and Hardwick Avenues. This family supplied all the butter and milk to their immediate neighbors.

Partial Solution to Water Difficulties Found . . .

The Piedmont Land Company directors were finding it increasingly necessary to devise some means of getting the water from the Contra Costa pipe on Vernal Avenue up to the higher levels. On the knoll which today is bounded by Scenic and Blair Avenues a circular reservoir was made, and into it water was pumped by a small coal-and-wood burning engine. But what it lacked in size this engine more than compensated for in noise. It was located on the southeast corner of the Wright place. So this family became responsible for fueling the steam boiler and keeping the supply tank above filled with water at all times. To accomplish this, the small Worcester cottage was moved up the hill closer to the covered cistern, and in the adjoining garden another, more spacious bungalow was built. On this gorgeous location one had an unobstructed view westward. Mr. Worcester and his Chinese servant occupied this larger house, while the old cottage still served as classroom for the Bowman children.

Advent of Hugh Craig ...

It is easy to see how the Piedmont Land Company encouraged a high standard of home-building for this particular section of Alameda County and how they managed to prompt others of similar suburban tastes to purchase their properties. Hugh Craig is the next name to be recorded on a Piedmont Land Company map. During 1879 my father purchased two parcels of land, comprising in all six acres between Vernal and Mountain Avenues.

Mr. Bigelow, director of the land company, and Craig were friends in San Francisco, where both had business interests on California Street. On Saturdays Mr. Bigelow would often accompany the Craig family for a scenic drive out into the hills. In springtime with locust trees in fragrant bloom and fields covered with the brilliant orange of poppies and purple of the lupin, the temptation of having a home there, plus some excellent salesmanship, proved too great, and my father and mother were eager purchasers.

During the following year, an English-style home was constructed on the highest portion of the property in the center. Under the architectural direction of Samuel Newsome, the house showed the great prevalence of mill-work and decorative filigree so popular in this period. Thus in the summer of 1880 Hugh Craig brought his wife with Evelyn, Roy and baby Margery from the old Myrtle Street home up into this rural community.

The ingrained strains of a Scotch ancestry motivated the impelling determination in my father to see happy homes under a stable form of good government. "None was more active in promoting measures for the benefit of the city or state in general and of San Francisco and of Alameda County in particular. None was more interested in municipal affairs, even international in scope . . . His name was destined to become a familiar one throughout all the Piedmont region and to be perpetuated in the formation of the City which he loved . . ." (4)

During the next forty years Hugh Craig was a regular commuter to his California Street office in San Francisco, and, like most of the suburbanites, enjoyed those hours of enforced leisure spent in travelling to and from his work. On slow cars, trains and creaking ferry-boats these busy men read the morning newspapers, gathered in knots to discuss the local or national topics, or grouped together to exchange the latest tid-bits of neighborhood gossip.

Eucalyptus Trees Color the Landscape . . .

Yet another digression from the actors in the story to its setting now leads to the familiar and picturesque eucalyptus trees which have become so common throughout the Bay Area, especially in Piedmont. Although there is no record extant of precisely when this first species of eucalypti came into the United States, it would seem probable that the first trees were grown in San Francisco by a Mr. Walker from seeds brought to him from Australia by some sea-faring friend about 1855. Probably Walter Blair heard of this new horticultural venture and passed the news on to his brother William. For, as already stated, William commenced at this time a nursery enterprise in which he specialized in these seedlings.

With these sturdy young trees the Blairs forested many local hills. They were also used as property dividing lines, for the ranchers discovered that they made excellent wind-breaks. A double row of these seedlings was planted along the fenceline of the Mountain View Cemetery. These made rapid progress, having been carefully tended and hand-watered during their infant years. In the past seventy years travelers up and down Moraga Road have admired their stately grandeur, and it was with universal feelings of regret that they were removed in 1936 for the widening and modernization of the highway.

"Nature in Australia had but little in the way of variety with which to work, so she took the eucalyptus and proceeded to ring all the changes she could in difference of appearance." The blue-gum (eucalyptus globulus) is perhaps the most common genus seen in California. The leaves are so delicately hung that they allow much sunlight to filter through. If one is looking for sylvan tracery, all that is necessary is some of these blue-gum saplings planted against a plain

(4) From *Alameda County History.*

Mr. and Mrs. I. L. Requa—1880

white wall. The simplicity of the landscape gardening at the San Fran-francisco World's Fair in 1915 made full use of this effect. Gums are most appealing when young; as one writer has remarked, they some-times show remarkable bravery: "One of the most courageous sights I have seen was a white gum sapling growing on a ledge in the red walls of a gorge in central Australia, a young thing still green and graceful, standing in the face of a six years' drought."

One outstanding specimen of magnificent grandeur stood straight and stalwart before the gateway to the Piedmont Springs Hotel grounds. This gigantic eucalyptus was our pride for over a decade, a stately landmark, until within the past few years, the leaves slowly shrivelled and dropped with no new ones to replace the old. Life was fast ebbing away. The heavy street paving had encroached too far, and the tree was deprived of sufficient moisture. So the park authorities relegated this hardy old monarch to firewood and ashes, and with its passing a period was put to the era into which our story now enters. However, a famous California artist, Xavier Martinez, has perpet-uated for posterity the sublime majesty of the eucalypti. His paintings of them are of great beauty and are highly prized.

Increasing Sense of Unity . . .

The bonds of common interests between the people who lived on Piedmont Avenue and those few who lived in the heights above were brought more closely together with the increasing number of children. Any history of this section from the year 1880 through 1894 must give recognition to the dominating personality of Mrs. Amy C. Horton, who was a teacher of remarkable ability. She was an austere and com-manding woman from New England and quickly assumed a position of leadership when the new Piedmont school-house was built. How-ever, the earliest local primary group owes its start to Mrs. Annie Raymond Hume, who used the living room of her home as the first public school in Piedmont. This large house was built during the sev-enties, in the center of the tract just north of the present school prop-erty. Her three oldest children, Lizzie, Frank and May, were in need of some type of instruction, and the original idea grew until eleven pupils were gathered in attendance for that first class. This was just prior to 1875, and it was held in the sort of social hall in the basement of the Hume home. Mrs. Hume contributed towards the salary of the teacher.

The school zone included at that time the district from Telegraph Avenue to Trestle Glen and from Twenty-Sixth Street out to the Moraga hills. It required a lot of persuasive speech to convince some residents within this sparsely settled region that a school was an important necessity. Finally, in 1876 the County purchased the lot to the south of the William Blair home and nursery. This piece of land had a two-hundred foot frontage on Piedmont Avenue and extended back up the slope as far as the trail now known as Howe Street. On the south side of this property was a corner saloon with latticed swing-doors and benches along the outside wall on which the over-inebriated often spent the night after the doors were locked. The Junction had achieved popularity for itself, and the drivers of the passing teams were prone to drop in for a "quick one".

Description of the School House . . .

The school-house design was square with two front entrances opening into a single large room, each entrance approached by equally steep stairs. Through the windows of the rear anteroom the eagle eyes of Mrs. Horton could watch with equal assiduity, behavior in both the boys' and girls' divisions of the yard during recess and lunch periods. To each of her ever-increasing brood she gave individual and personal attention and taught alone the three r's she considered essential throughout the entire eight grades. In one subject was she devoid of knowledge. During the singing lessons she had to resort to the "tune-pipe", and from that point the children carried on with no assistance from their non-musical leader. The songs sometimes sounded rather discordant, but Mrs. Horton went on oblivious.

Some Poignant Memories Recalled . . .

Mrs. Horton was the wife of Professor Horton, principal of the Lincoln School in Oakland. Both were educators of high scholastic caliber and came from the rock-bound coast of Maine, where as a foundation for all learning children were taught the qualities of truthfulness, honesty and obedience for the essential cornerstone of the rest of their education. With all of her mental and physical abilities this wonderful woman tried to inculcate these principles into the very mixed group of boys and girls set before her.

Arithmetic, spelling and grammar were stressed as of the greatest importance, and some of those poor country boys had their sums beaten into their heads with the most forceful methods. A riding whip hung just inside Mrs. Horton's anteroom door, and anyone failing or disobeying a rule knew that his legs would soon be tingling. At these tragic moments little girls of the class often burst into tears of fright as well as of sympathy.

Among the few who went down from the hills to this school were Luita Booth, Todd, Edith, and Guy Lilliencrantz, Evelyn, Roy and Margery Craig. As often as the weather permitted, we carried our lunch-baskets and walked the mile and a quarter along Vernal to Moraga, then down the path leading between those two rows of eucalyptus trees next to the cemetery fence. On bleak, wintry mornings the hired man would collect all the children to drive us down in the carriage. Occasionally when our coaxings prevailed we had the enormous thrill of riding the exciting trip on Martin Miller's horse-car line, catching the eight o'clock car. Our parents did not care for this arrangement, however, as it afforded too much time to dawdle in front of the Junction saloon.

A blacksmith shop on the opposite corner had great fascination for some of the boys before and after classes. The pounding and reshaping of broken horse-shoes on the anvils made interesting entertainment. It was always a busy place with several horses tied inside awaiting their turn to be shod, and the owners of private carriage animals had to make appointments in advance if they wanted immediate attention.

Popular Equine Personalities ...

Mention might be made here of the horse, for he was such an essential and integral part of family life. For example, the Requas had in their stables a most perfectly matched pair of cinnamon brown trotters to do the carriage chores. A familiar sight on those red-rock roads would be John, the family coachman, driving the well-groomed team, decorated in their nickel-plated harness, and the shining black "rockaway" with Mrs. Requa sitting with erect dignity in the rear seat. Her gracious smile was always ready for those of us whom she met or passed on the long drive into Oakland.

Mr. and Mrs. Booth drove about in their low-slung phaeton with its fringe around the covered top, and in winter some side curtains could be buttoned on. Their horse was very gentle with a slow and laborious gait. Mr. Booth was regarded with great affection by the children, for he served as a member of the board of trustees for the first Piedmont school and it portended a joyful interlude when the pupils saw him pulling up in front of the school to pay a call upon Mrs. Horton and her eight grades.

Chinese Labor in Piedmont ...

The Chinese of the eighties occasionally added a note of exotic color along the Avenue and up Moraga way. There was felt at this time a general antipathy toward the great number of Chinese brought into the regions along the Pacific Coast who were used as cheap, coolie laborers. Their history during these years is full of fury, noise, commotion and confused California legislation. This latter was often construed to benefit some special interests at the expense of the helpless Chinese. Here may be traced the thread of subtle selfishness centuries old tangling through these years into the present economic turmoil.

From the behavior of a small group of children on their early walks to the Junction school one could observe the attitude of rancor and prejudice that permeated the feelings of the general populace toward the Chinese in the 1880's. Each morning these youngsters would meet the local Oriental vegetable man who wore his neatly braided queue three feet down his back and balanced across his slight shoulders a flat hickory pole to which was attached at either end the handles of a huge round bamboo basket. These baskets were fitted with deep trays which were crammed with fruit, berries and vegetables, as the season permitted, always picked garden fresh. The little Chinese gardener carried this double burden which would make a white man stagger under the load, but he maintained a steady dog trot pace that allowed him to cover the ground without expending too much energy.

The Chinese grew their produce on the San Francisco side of the Bay, and those vendors who wished to sell to people in Oakland or out beyond would have to start prior to daybreak, crossing the Bay by the Creek Route Ferry to First and Broadway and from there keep up their steady trot out for miles on devious and rough roads to serve their regular customers. These routes were certainly not made any more pleasant by the presence of small boys who took fiendish delight in hurling stones and epithets at these unassuming Orientals. Incidents such as this occurred frequently on the Moraga path and was the cause of great terror among the little girls accompanying the stone casters. Sometimes the patience of the persecuted vegetable man would snap, and he would manage to extricate himself from the tangle of spilled baskets in time to make a quick dash after his juvenile tormentors, who with their nimble feet usually managed to evade his vengeance. One tragic example of this period of wanton cruelty lived in Oakland for a number of years; a faithful cleaning boy worked by the day in the homes of some of the "best families", and grew to be an old man, totally blind in one eye, due to the accuracy of a small boy's sling-shot.

Chinese Help . . .

The help problems were few in those days because of the great numbers of Chinese immigrants. They were pliable servants and marvelous cooks; their cakes and pastries were unrivaled in the finest *patisseries*. Those working in the homes of the elite wore their glossy black hair in long queues dangling down their backs, often bringing some variety into the coiffure by braiding a length of brilliant shaded ribbon in the end. Frequently they wore their native costumes, made with soft silks and stiff brocades; for streetwear they would add a little black pillbox hat set off by a red glass cherry on top.

However, few Piedmont families were staffed by resident Chinese; they usually were called in for "extras" of housecleaning. Only Mr. and Mrs. Wing on Mountain Avenue had a permanent Chinese houseboy, Tuie, whose later life has been spent in Piedmont. Tuie made himself an inseparable part of the early history of the community.

Colorful and Spectacular Funerals . . .

Everything always seemed bright and gay about the Chinese, even their funerals. When the departed one who was the focal point of the honor was rated high among his fellow men, the funeral procession was exceedingly long as it wound its way out Piedmont Avenue. One could almost measure the prestige of the departed soul by the length of the cortege. The hour for these colorful proceedings always seemed to fall at the time that school was out, about mid-afternoon. A huge, awe-inspiring dragon preceded the much decorated horses. The rude caisson would follow, succeeded by the plodding train of woeful mourners who emitted weird chants and scattered scarlet leaflets along the route, in order to ward off evil spirits. Into the cemetery and over to the Chinese section this motley crowd went, leaving behind them a splendid feast at the graveside to pacify any spirits lurking about. But it has been whispered that the mourners were not above fortifying themselves from the generous supplies of roast meats, candy, cigars and other means of solace placed for the use of the soul on his way to the heavenly kingdom, as well as for the pacification of spirits.

Though the price of watching these fascinating operations would be a harsh tongue-lashing by an anxious mother or perhaps a more graphic type of lashing by an irate father, the belated children plodding wearily up the hill after one of these affairs felt that the price was worth it. The spectacle of the procession warranted any heated aftermath.

Difficulties Encountered in Construction ...

It might be well to pause at this point in the narrative to envision the patience, time and labor consumed in the erection of these homes. The mansions built preceding the Craig home were constructed under the supervision of San Francisco architects and contractors. Along the Oakland estuary westward from Washington Street were located the lumber yards and contractors' supply materials. From here to the Highlands the distance was almost six miles, with a rise of over three hundred feet.

One team of heavy, powerful work-horses would draw the load of brick or sand out Broadway, then up Piedmont Avenue, as far as the foot of the Moraga grade at Pleasant Valley Road. Here the driver and the team awaited the arrival of the second relief wagon. When both drivers had partaken of some mild refreshment at the Junction saloon, they proceeded to take the fresh pair of horses from the second wagon and hitched them to the single tree in front of the first team. Then with cracking whips and much oral encouragement, the weary but willing animals started the load up the steep slopes ahead. The driver of the lead horses walked beside them, handling his own reins and exercising his cruel whip which was frequently laid on most brutally, especially if the road happened to be muddy and wet, for when the wagon was halted, a terrific struggle ensued to get it started again.

During the eighties great loads of lumber, brick and sand were hauled in this manner, and often several laden wagons were seen standing at the foot of the grade, while six horses were dragging up an extra heavy load. These same faithful beasts had to make a second and sometimes a third arduous trip on the same day. Such labor must have been costly, even in those days when twenty dollar gold-pieces could be spread so far.

Last Large Tract of Piedmont
Land Company Holdings . . .

Again we revert to the heights where the thread of the Piedmont story continues. Here on the grounds of these early homes small vegetable gardens provided some of the family needs. The hints of change, however, were steadily growing more distinct. The last large tract of the Piedmont Land Company's holding, fenced in by a triple layer of board rails, extended easterly from Vernal Avenue to the trail at the edge of the eucalyptus forest, now Scenic Avenue. This almost level field lay between the Craig acreage on the southern boundary and what had been the Blair lands to the north. Mr. Bigelow had permitted his friend, Hugh Craig, to have the use of this idle land to plant a grain crop, and in return for this Father paid the County taxes on the property. Because it was quite an acreage, the crop was usually large, but it required a lot of hay to feed each year two horses, three cows and nearly always a calf. A Mr. Gray, who owned and farmed a sizeable place over in the Thornhill district, would arrive each fall, bringing along team and equipment to do the plowing, harrowing and seeding for the following season.

The men walked briskly and lightly over the newly turned earth, scattering handfuls of oats or barley from the heavy sacks slung across their shoulders. A second harrowing immediately followed this sowing, because were it not done quickly flocks of sparrows and robins would descend upon the field. Hawks, too, were numerous and bold to the extreme, darting down after tender young chickens and turkeys when they strayed out from the protective coops. It took about six weeks before the thick green carpet of fresh sprouts appeared over the grain field. By the approach of spring these seedlings had grown high enough for us to play an active game of hide-and-seek among the ripening stalks, when we climbed over the fence.

Again, with a noisy reaper heralding his arrival, Mr. Gray drove his "outfit" to the gate on Vernal Avenue. This horse-drawn machine went around the field in diminishing circles until the tall grain lay flat. There the sweet mown stalks lay for days, drying out in the hot sun, before the rakers arrived to gather them into those little "cocks". Then, after another few weeks' seasoning, these small piles were put into one huge, oblong stack to await the men and horses who came with a heavy piece of machinery called the baler. When each bale had been sufficiently stamped down by the men's feet, the team of horses added

Viewing *The Highlands* (from *Lakeshore Ave.*) —1884

their pressure by pulling on the windlass chains. With the hay finally in bales it was then loaded on the wagons and hauled over to the Craig barn, where the men hoisted it by block and tackle up through a sliding door into the large hayloft above.

Remainder of the Craig Property ...

The regular cowbarns, located on the rear slope behind the stable, were generally filled with the unbaled hay from the Craigs' own fields. Down through the orchard of peach, apricot, plum and cherry trees lay a wide path, bordered by sunflowers. Some of the tall stems produced such huge yellow flowers that the ripening seeds made the blossom drop heavily. These were allowed to dry out until the arrival of fall, when the hired hand would cut them down a few at a time and toss them into the turkey yard, where a flock of cackling young birds were being fattened for the winter dinner table.

But the peaceful pastoral existence was soon to disappear, to be replaced by the more varied phase of human activity that came with increased population.

Changes Appearing in Piedmont ...

When Mr. and Mrs. Fred Whitney, the first managers of the Piedmont Springs Hotel, gave up their position, the place went into the hands of William Plitt. Something had evidently gone wrong with the original financing, but this man, who had held a like office in an East Oakland hotel, had the money and German thrift to enable the Piedmont Hotel to continue in existence for a few years longer. The saloon on the ground floor still did a flourishing business. However, many undesirable characters, both men and women, were noisily frequenting this lovely residential section. This state of affairs caused great concern to many of its citizens, among them Hugh Craig, who began agitating for the revocation of the County liquor license, not a very popular task. With the saloon down at the Junction and this one further up the grade many things might happen in that sparsely settled suburb. Small wonder each householder kept a loaded revolver handy and carried it with him on any lonely night drives.

Coincident with these changes, the Liliencrantz family decided to move back into Oakland, where their growing children would be closer to the schools and could make a wider number of social contacts. When the Bowmans discarded their big house at Hillside and Magnolia to move up to the Worcester cottage, their former estate was taken over for a few years by Jesse Grant, son of the Civil War general, and his family. Reportedly, the famous ex-president of the United States was entertained in this home when he visited San Francisco.

The young Grants' interest in the East Bay was doubtless due to the desire of the attractive wife to be near her parents, Mr. and Mrs. Chapman. Mr. Chapman and the senior Edson Adams had been co-owners of the extensive waterfront lands along the Oakland estuary. The elder daughter of Jesse Grant married John Mason, scion of a distinguished San Francisco family. Mr. Mason and his wife added to the eclat of the period by driving in their high, single-seated buggy behind a pair of spirited thoroughbreds from Alameda over into the Piedmont hills. The only child of this couple, Florence Mason, was a college friend of the author's at the University of California and was married in 1902 at the cathedral in Calcutta to the distinguished British engineer. Sir Fredrick Palmer. The English Government honored him for his outstanding services in the construction of bridges throughout India.

Two Fires Bring Fame ...

But the lovely Grant estate was not long occupied by that family, and soon after they left, a fire, blazing suddenly into the darkness of the night, completely demolished that handsome and costly residence. It is not known what caused the flames, but because of the total lack of water and engines everything perishable went up in the holocaust.

Another blaze occurred about the same time, or perhaps a year later; the exact date has not been definitely established. It happened on New Year's Day, either 1886 or 1887. The Craigs, accompanied by Grandmother Gilcrest, drove down to Oakland to celebrate the holiday by a family dinner at the home of Uncle Frank Gilcrest on Linden Street. In the late afternoon we started the homeward journey. The horse was permitted to choose his own pace on the trip up the hill, when around a particularly sharp bend in the road the Oakland fire engine appeared. The spent and weary team of grays seemed glad to halt as the men with accompanying gestures gave a graphic description of their futile experiences. Fire had demolished the once-famed Piedmont Hotel to its foundations. Appeals for assistance had been flashed to Oakland, but even when urged to the breaking point, these powerful horses could not get the heavy and bulky engine over the five-mile pull in time to attempt to compete with the onslaught of the blaze, especially with the insufficient water supply and little pressure. At this exciting news we were all astounded and regretted having missed such a colorful spectacle. However, Father's surprise was tempered by his feeling of elation over this providential removal of the blot on the center of the otherwise ideal home district. After a light touch of the whip Sorrel was urged to continue the pull up to the Springs, where smoldering ashes and three blackened chimneys remained to tell of the past glories of the Piedmont Hotel.

Once again, through the publicity given to these fires, Piedmont in embryo, received attention from many who were destined to become future citizens. Those who were living at this time on Brush, Castro and Adeline Streets, some from the fashionable Lake Merritt district and others from the East Oakland and Fruitvale districts of the social elite, all came up during those crisp winter days to view the ruins and to search for the site of future homes. (5)

Recorded on the maps of Piedmont as early as 1883 is the well-known name of George E. Wheaton as the purchaser of that block of land bounded by Oakland, Hillside, Vista and Bonita Avenues. If the original aim of the owner was to build a home here, such an idea did not materialize. Evidently, the gay social life of their Lake Street menage was more appealing to the tastes of the sons, George and "Brick", and the daughter Elisabeth. The young belle of Oakland later was married to Edson F. Adams, and since they have lived in their mansion on Sea View Avenue, they have given Piedmont much of its outstanding social distinction and glitter.

Illumination Facilities . . .

The very important problem of the water and gas was an all-absorbing one on those early Piedmont estates. Well impressed on my youthful mind was the much quoted price of water paid by my father; it was one dollar for every thousand gallons. Needless to say, such an amount did not stretch very far when it had to serve a family of four children, three servants, two horses, a couple of cows and always a pen with three young pigs. These latter had to have their wallow, even at the expense of the children, who had to be content with a semi-weekly bath, often "two in a tub"! Then the expanse of green lawn called for its irrigation, as did the flower beds and the all-year vegetable garden. One can easily imagine how the water bill grew to

---

(5) Cf. Appendix II for these names.

forbidding proportions in the ordinary household budget. Gas for illumination had been distributed through Oakland, but no extension had yet been made to the hills above.

Except for the Requa estate, where their private gas machine supplied the big house, servants' quarters and the barns with light, the rest of the families still kept their coal-oil lamps hanging from ceiling centers and gently raised or lowered them by brass chains running over pulleys. They seemed very elegant to childish eyes with those moss roses encircling the white china shades and crystal prisms dangling below. There were also many smaller lamps which required daily refilling. Then the tallow candles which needed particular care or they would drip messily over the carrier and the small coal-oil lanterns already described completed the lighting facilities in the average Piedmont home of the eighties.

Carriages also had to have their road lights, square side lanterns with extended candle holders. These were kept in constant readiness for the frequent evening drives into Oakland for some social function, usually a musical gathering. On those dark nights travel was slow and tedious over the sinister miles of unlighted roads, and a loaded pistol, short and stubby, was conveniently placed under the front seat; Father called it an English gun. Apparently he and Mother had some lurking premonition of a hold-up occurring, especially along the steep climb where the double row of eucalyptus trees paralleled the highly boarded cemetery fence.

Intricate Burglar Alarm System ...

However, their fears were not idle, for strange things did occur out in these suburbs. Our house was equipped with the standard burglar alarm system: brass springs installed within the window casings and if the sash were lowered below this spring the warning bell immediately started to ring in the master bedroom. Here the indicator box was located, and from the box the brave parent could read the exact spot of the thief's attempted entrance. With this intricate and expensive mechanism, as far as I can recall, the sole alarms ever rung were caused by careless servants trying to get more circulation of air into the room on a warm night.

The Requa mansion had its alarm system on an even more elaborate scale. The butler, George Washington, a tall, courteous mulatto, was delegated to check the location of any alarm signal. A dread of burglars seemed to permeate those peaceful hills.

A Natural Wonder ...

Occasionally a winter storm of unusual force and intensity provided an exciting episode. For example, on the morning of February 6, 1887, a great scenic transformation had taken place and winter wonderland was created. Nature had covered the entire countryside with a pure white carpet, and rudely improvised sleds were seen coasting down the Piedmont roads. Thick ice had to be broken on all the water troughs throughout the district. Quite a number of residents drove into Mountain View Cemetery and up its main driveway, just to inspect for themselves the solid circles of icicles which had formed around the fountain that ordinarily was such a lovely sight of flowing waters.

Captain Lawrence ...

But this event was just a freak of nature, and for the most part, community life went along at an even pace. Rural simplicity and friendliness contributed much to the intimacy of neighbors during those years, and people took their leisure by slower modes of travel. The depression of the early nineties forced a few of the residents to move away, but others soon came to fill in vacancies. One of these newcomers who deserve mention was the enthralling Captain Lawrence from New England.

Off the rocky coast of Massachussetts on the island of Nantucket, William H. Lawrence was born in 1825. After a colorful career on the sea William became a ship-master in his own right on the Atlantic Coast and then married Miss Chase, the eldest of four sisters whose family he frequently visited in their Cape Cod home. Captain Lawrence and his young wife took passage, via the Isthmus of Panama, to San Francisco, where he was superintendent of the United States Bonded Warehouses.

During 1882 he resigned his position and bought a home in the Piedmont hills. This modest house, later known as 305 Vernal Avenue, had been erected and occupied only a short time by the Wrights. Their estate on Hardwick Avenue passed into other hands soon after the Bowman financial crisis and collapse. Forced by his wife's critical asthmatic condition to find a milder climate, Captain Lawrence sought to find relief for her across the Bay in Piedmont. Possibly, they were also influenced by their friendship with Mr. Worcester in their decision to become part of the hillside community. For the succeeding thirty years, they were included in the growth of the city about them.

The Craig Home—1882-1891

Children were the first to succumb to the fascinations of the lovable sea captain, and they would gather in his basement shop on wintry days, where the little stove gave its flickering light and warmth to the high, spacious room. Youngsters would quietly sit and watch him making those tiny little fishing boats, miniature wildmills and weathervanes and listened to his tales of Cape Cod in the hey-day of the clipper ships and of the village people who had carved out a life for themselves along its rocky shores. As newer families came to these parts, they too soon learned the joy of dropping in to see the Lawrences. Often they might be carrying a basket of fruit from the orchard or a pat of fresh butter if the churning had been especially good.

Interchange of Produce Among the Families . . .

Then in due time would arrive the season for sending the pigs to market. Most of these estates kept a quota of three pigs through the season of growth, when they thrived on skim milk and the swill from the kitchen. No garbage trucks climbed those hills, nor were they needed.

McDermott would come up from his butcher shop at the Junction with his wagon and men, usually his two sons, to slaughter the hogs. During those hours of blood and horror our family always went off in the carriage. On the following day there would be returned to the household the prepared head of one of these porkers out of which developed the pressed mold of head cheese. Delicious sandwiches were made from the well seasoned delicacy for the school lunch baskets on succeeding days.

One of the pigs was always returned in dressed form to serve for family use, while the selling price of the other two helped defray the figures on the current month's butcher bill. The hams and bacons were smoked, whole shoulders and other portions were salted down in a large barrel kept in the coolest part of the basement. Sometimes a selected roast went with compliments to the Lawrences and another to the Liliencrantz family, who in their turn would present some choice fruits or fowl in season.

Changes in the Lawrence Menage . . .

In later years the Richardsons, Sharons and Berkenfelds joined the Wings and the Craigs in the giving of a friendly wave to the tiny, smiling face of Mrs. Lawrence as she sat in her rocker peering from the front parlor window. To her it seemed a sad day when Martin

Miller and his bob-tailed car ceased the hourly trips on Vernal Avenue. Her chair soon appeared at the side kitchen window from which she nodded greetings at neighbors as they waited on the platform for the new cable cars. However, the familiar face appeared in the framework of rose-vines for only a few years longer; then the frail hand was stilled forever.

After a brief lapse of time the vacant chair was soon filled by either of the Misses Chase, Susan or Rebecca, whom Captain Lawrence had invited some years previously to come from Cape Cod to make their home in Piedmont. They lived on with him after the death of his wife as his housekeepers until his own death in 1910.

The income which had been left to these two elderly spinsters must have been extremely meager, yet the pride of family and past position was so ingrained that their closest neighbors were unaware of their acute state of poverty and loneliness. It was not until one morning when George Merras, who rented a room in their home, detected an odor of gas and found them in the kitchen seated in the accustomed rockers with unlighted gas jets turned on full, that the evidence became painfully clear. Such was the tragic finale of these two gentle women. Truly it is a sorry blot upon the escutcheon of Piedmont that such sorrow could have existed amid surroundings of wealth. A warmer spirit of Christian neighborliness would have made such a tragedy impossible.

The Myers Bring the Echo of Carnegie ...

The name of Andrew Carnegie deserves a place in the Piedmont annals during the late eighties and into the early nineties. A daughter, Frances Carnegie, wife of William Myers, bought the southwest corner of Oakland and Hillside Avenues in 1885. Mr. Myers was a great horse fancier, and as there is nothing authentic to inform us as to the reason these young people chose to build in this undeveloped section, one might imagine that perhaps they wished to escape the sandy trails and cobbled streets of San Francisco. On the hills sloping up from the East Bay they could drive for miles over old Spanish trails which had been modernized to the extent that they had been broadened and paved with red rock.

Finest construction and exquisite hard wood panelling went into the Myers house. An architect from the eastern United States must have been employed as the facade indicated a style not yet adopted around the Bay Region. Sandstone from some distant part had to be hauled up the steep roads and formed the deep foundation and the broad chimneys. The interior finish consisted of choice burl redwood in wide panels in effective places, such as side-walls and doors. Seventy oil lamps were used for lighting purposes. Hung about the rooms were many valuable paintings and tapestries, among them a famous and magnificent piece, *A Reading from Homer*. An unobstructed view over the Bay could be had from the western windows.

On the lower southeastern corner of the estate stood a stable for trained race horses and fast trotters. Even the individual stalls were constructed of hard wood, with thick, soft padding over the framework. Mr. Myers and his son were often seen speeding along Vernal Avenue in a fancy equipage, driving a perfectly matched pair of thoroughbreds. Seldom did Mrs. Myers appear, nor was she ever known to return any of the annual or semi-annual calls exchanged among the ladies of the neighborhood.

Sudden Departure and Subsequent Fire ...

This family suddenly and without warning departed from Piedmont, and the artistic house was left vacant. In 1895, however, this desirable corner was purchased from a bank by Dr. A. F. Merriman who soon moved out with his family from Oakland. But one night in April, 1896, a fire roared its way up from the basement, forcing the frightened occupants to flee from the house in nightrobes, some even minus a slipper so hasty was their evacuation. The tumult of the flames and the bright glow which illuminated the whole sky soon had all the young Craigs joining the race across to the panic-stricken Merriman and Thomas clans. The hour was weird (one thirty in the morning), cable cars had ceased to run, and communications and assistance were unavailable. The flames and heat were intense, and the work of destruction was rapid. A bedraggled group of people trudged up to the Craigs' for comfort, coffee and a few hours' troubled rest on couches and improvised beds. News of the disaster spread, and soon neighbors were trooping up with donations of food and clothing. Mrs. Fannie Thomas tells of a large hamper sent by Mrs. Bowman containing grand satin ball gowns, vintage of the eighties, boned and be-ruffled, with stiff high collars.

Amusement and laughter helped to dissipate momentarily the sadder, tragic aspects of the situation. There had been no insurance on the house with its lavish furnishings and priceless interior. But the same solid stone foundation was used when in 1900 the Merriman family rebuilt and returned to become active in the growth of the hill town, and were among the founders of the Piedmont Community Church.

Randall Family Take Over the Lilliencrantz Estate ...

The departure of Dr. Lilliencrantz and his family to Oakland from their home at Vernal Avenue and Hazel Lane, left those lovely gardens neglected for only a short time. Almost immediately thereafter, carpenters and laborers were making extensive improvements: adding a third story to the already spacious dwelling, improving the barns and outbuildings in readiness to care for the horses, cows, pigs and chickens and finally building the customary dog kennels.

In 1888 after all these preparations had been completed, the Charles W. Randall family moved over from San Francisco and became yet another acquisition to the sparsely settled Piedmont community. We Craigs were particularly delighted to have Mary and Marion to visit and play with Margery and me, while the two sons, Charlie and Eddie paired off with the younger Craig boys, Colin and Eric. The Randalls had a wonderful playroom filled with toys of every description, and at Christmas their tree glittered with gifts the like of which Santa Claus had never brought to the Craig children.

Mrs. Randall and the nurses did much to make the young friends welcome with tea parties and garden picnics. The school student body, however, was not swelled by this family; the Randall children had their own private governess, so they lost out on those early morning rambles down to the Piedmont school.

Mr. Randall was a daily commuter to San Francisco to the Wakelee Drug Stores. He was the principal owner of these stores and also had patent rights for that famous cosmetic, "Camelline for the Complexion". Quite a fortune had been amassed through the advertising and sales of this early beauty cream.

Wild Life in the Neighborhood ...

Occasionally Father would join us youngsters in a tramp over the hills where we would race ahead to seek out the first flowers of the season or linger behind watching the quail scurrying at the mother's querulous call. One Sunday my father took us through the present St. James Wood section, when without warning he halted suddenly.

On the knoll directly in front of us stood a majestic California mountain lion. Unobtrusively but quickly we removed ourselves from his sphere. Though these animals had been observed in this region before but had caused no damage, we took no chances.

Often we heard the eerie call of the coyotes at night, and wild cats were frequent visitors, coming close enough to home farms to steal any chicken that had strayed from the coop. However, the barking of the dogs usually kept the wilder animals at a safe distance, and the only real pests were the skunks which might sneak in too close at times.

Stock Reversals Hit the Bowmans . . .

Although the Bowman family were close neighbors, their children were not among the small coterie from the hill section who attended the Junction School under the strict tutelage of Mrs. Horton. Those early morning saunterings down to the schoolhouse might have been livelier and more adventurous if the numbers could have been increased by Arthur, Alice, Adelaide, Harry, Frankie and Natalie Bowman. However, their education progressed under the guidance of a private tutor, Joseph Worcester. On occasion, though, the youngsters came into the Craig gardens to play, and Roy and I were sometimes invited to the elegantly equipped play yard and nursery of the Bowmans.

According to historical records, the boom days in San Francisco began to have their aftermath in the late eighties and there were frequent financial failures. This period of slight depression struck with particular force upon those who had over-extended their speculative investments. Lands, mines and wheat futures were favorite ventures. Mr. Bowman had been successful as an investor of funds for San Francisco people, largely among the women, to whom he had sold Piedmont Land Company bonds. Then came the crash on the San Francisco Mining Exchange. Overnight the Bowmans had lost everything.

As the sudden reverses befell many in San Francisco, so the repercussions were felt by many on both sides of the Bay. Their lovely estate on Magnolia Avenue was vacated, and the entire Bowman family moved up into the Worcester cottage. The great retinue of servants, along with the string of fine horses and carriages, disappeared from the Piedmont scene. Mr. Worcester removed his own living quarters and extensive library across the garden from the larger house to the smaller cottage, which had been used as the school room.

Only a short time elapsed after this crash until the death of Mr. Bowman. From this point onward, the elder son and daughters displayed their oustanding ability to carry on and always attended with touching solicitude the semi-invalid mother, who remained so lovely and gentle.

With this family atop the hill a path was soon carved out from the Craig side fence across the grain field, covering what is now Oakland Avenue, and then on to the dusty or muddy trail through the Bowman-Worcester orchard. Atop this knoll and to the side of the cottages loomed the high, wooden circular fence surrounding the reservoir which supplied water to the properties above Vernal Avenue.

Much interest and controversy centered about a small pump house at the northeast corner of Blair and Hardwick Avenues. From this point the water had to be lifted to the supply tank above. Alan Wright and Arthur Bowman shoveled many tons of coal into that hungry engine to hold the steam gauge up to the pumping point. Whenever Roy disappeared from the Craig place, he could generally be found at the engine house, blackened by coal dust, but happy in his chosen role as assistant stoker to the older "fellers".

The Wright family resided in the large house just below the Worcester place. Mr. Wright kept the cows that supplied both families with milk, and from the thick and carefully skimmed cream the women churned the home-made butter. As mentioned before, Mrs. Bowman and Mrs. Wright were sisters. One of the Wright daughters, Miss Bertha, has been recognized for her leadership in formulating plans for the establishment of the East Bay General Hospital, known now as Children's Hospital. She served for many years as the supervising nurse of this institution and was retired with honor.

Social Whirl in Piedmont . . .

The matrons, who observed strictly the social customs of the period, had engraved upon their calling cards the day of the week that they were at home for the reception of guests. Thus, despite the fact that their lives might have been circumscribed with the rearing of comparatively large families and the various domestic chores weighing down upon the director of these busy households, the social amenities were never lost sight of or forgotten. Mrs. Requa, for example, kept every Wednesday afternoon free and many carriages and phaetons, with liveried coachmen and foam bespattered horses, entered the gateway between its black and gold pillars. They drove through the beautifully laid out garden to the front steps, where the ladies alighted. Mounting this broad staircase, they were met at the door by the butler, who ushered them into one of the parlors where the hostess graciously stepped forward to greet her guests. Such were the pleasant, informal gatherings which drew the women of the community together in bright chatter.

A frequent caller on those "Wednesdays" was Miss Mollie Connors, who was so full of life and gaiety, that she had the reputation of being on speaking terms with "everybody who was anybody". The *Saturday Night* paper which she edited in Oakland included upon its subscription list all the names with any social rating at all.

At Home on a Less Grand Scale . . .

My mother observed "first and third Thursdays". The parlor on those days was decorated with flowers and the second girl was held in readiness to serve tea. Possibly a couple of friends might drive their buggies up the graveled roadway, hitching the horses to a round topped post which was situated at the edge of the lawn opposite the front steps. Social life held small interest for this busy mother of six growing girls and boys, along with the large property which she personally supervised.

The pace and tone of development as a residential section of rare distinction was pretty much set during this period of the eighties. Quite inadvertently Piedmont had acquired that "magnificent background" referred to by home seekers in later years. These hills were reflecting similar scenes that were being enacted in and about many growing cities over the entire United States.

Past years had seen fortunes made and lost on the Mining Exchange or gathered into new hands through manipulation of stock transactions. Now other great estates were being amassed through new commercial enterprises, such as the putting into operation of the transcontinental railroad system. With these constructive builders of the West, whose aim it was to better conditions, came others with baser motives and ideals. For example, until the time that the Whitneys abandoned the Piedmont Hotel they had managed to maintain the high standards set by the directors of the Piedmont Land Company. But with the coming of another manager of the hotel, the personnel and guests soon changed into an imbibing and boisterous gathering, a fact which caused great annoyance to my father, for our home was just across a small field from this building. Sounds carried very clearly

The Meyers Home—1885

across the intervening territory. But, as already stated, a New Year's Day fire solved this knotty problem.

Experiments in Silk Culture . . .

Before leaving the period of the late eighties it might be well to describe a unique experiment that was held in this region. A lovely Sunday jaunt might take the ambitious hiker through some beautiful scenery. Starting with a turn off Vernal Avenue at Mountain, he would cross an old wooden bridge which spanned the deep creek at its bend, where Craig Avenue now cuts into Mountain. The important stream drained off a large watershed and continued down into the Springs grounds. On its banks grew dense patches of wild maiden-hair fern, while the delicate golden-back also grew in profusion. One of our favorite childhood pastimes was to meander down those steep banks in knee-high boots, just to see how far it was safe to venture. More than once the water came swelling over the boot-tops, or perhaps one of the more daring of the group would have to be pulled out of the slimy mud, a boot stuck behind him, unretrievable. Out from this wilderness of nature the visitors could drive up the narrow, twisting path, past the Wing estate and on around through the eucalyptus grove to the end of Mountain Avenue. Here on the rolling acres to the east stood an ugly, square two-story building. Over its doorway was fixed the inscription: United States Silk Culture Experimental Station.

W. B. Ewer of San Francisco assumed the management of this project, under the guidance and financial backing of the "Ladies Silk Culture Society of California". This organization was founded on January 2, 1885, as a successor to the "California Silk Culture Association". The principal object of the association was "to promote sericulture in the State of California by all practical means thereto". There is no evidence extant to prove that this organization really salvaged what was left of the industry in the state, but from that time there have been many other attempts to promote this singular process in the state.

This Piedmont venture received careful attention and must have required a large amount of capital investment. On the sloping land to the east down into Indian Gulch, as it was then called, Mr. Ewer had planted a mulberry orchard. The young trees grew rapidly and supplied the leaves on which the worms fed. During its years of operation the doors of this building were always open to the public. A full process of silk culture was demonstrated, from the hatching of the eggs through the six weeks of rapid worm growth and finishing with the weaving of the cocoons. This fascinating development was displayed in the daily stages of the worms' miraculous formation among the leaves and branches which had been placed over the worms as they began to spin their fibrous substance. In order to preserve the thread intact, the cocoons were given a bath of sulphur fumes to kill the live chrysalis within; otherwise, it would cut through the protecting cover and emerge as a heavy moth, ready to lay the eggs for another continuous life cycle.

Popularity of the Culture and a Personal Experience ...

The raising of silk-worms became a popular subject for school compositions, and many of us had our own little boxes of worms each spring. One season an attendant gave me a batch of eggs, the exact number is unknown. They were brought home and placed on a thin piece of cloth in a pasteboard box near the warmth of the kitchen stove. After a short lapse of time the tiny wriggling specks emerged, and, carefully following instructions, I covered them with a layer of finely cut mulberry leaves immediately. The rapid growth of the worms and their great consumption of leaves was an unforgettable sight. Much time was expended for their care and soon the entire household, including the servants, became involved. It was an interesting phenomenon that even worms can inspire affection in those caring for them. They are such good little beasts; they never crawl away, just raise their heads, an appealing look in their eyes, asking for food.

Instead of the fifty or more wrigglers that we had expected to feed from our mulberry tree, the batch had some 30,000 little wrigglers, all with ravenous mouths constantly opened to try to swallow the first bits of the frequent feedings. Growth was amazingly rapid, and Father bought a large, navy blue tent to erect over them in the garden, to soften the glaring light over their tiny eyes. Then a carpenter was called in to build redwood frames and tray racks with fine wire mesh bottoms, and this was my launching into the world of high business endeavor!

Importation of Mulberry Leaves ...

That was certainly a busy spring. We discovered to our dismay that the Silk Culture Farm, as the government experimental station was sometimes called, needed all of its own available leaves. But old Mr. Ewer encouraged the raising of these soft, white worms; so he made arrangements for sacks of mulberry leaves to be daily expressed to Oakland from San Mateo. Some members of the household would drive down to the Wells Fargo Express office in Oakland to pick them up every day.

Six weeks of feeding were required before completion of the period of growth. Then the spinning commenced. Branches were placed over the trays and the cocoons became so very thick among the leaves and twigs that the entire framework seemed, as one first entered the room, like a peek into fairyland. But when the end of those busy six weeks had been reached, the whole family was quite fed up with the experience.

Finally the little yellow balls of silk were gathered into sacks and taken up to the Silk Culture Farm for the last step, the sulphuring process. They were then weighed and sent to San Francisco for sale, the return being the large total of twenty-nine dollars (no income tax in those days!). With the pomp and circumstance due to the occasion my father solemnly delivered the cash into my hands, and at the earliest possible opportunity the money was spent at Mr. Lathrop's Jewelry Store on Broadway. Through his kindly advice the proud capitalist purchased a silver crumb tray which she presented with great pride and joy as a surprise for her dear mother. She well deserved that gift.

Ultimate Dissolution of the Business ...

Experiments, practiced over a decade of time, have proven the possibilities of silk culture in California. Climatic conditions are ideal, and mulberry leaves can be grown cheaply and in abundance. The price of labor, however, is abortive, and seems an insurmountable difficulty.

The venture in Piedmont survived for a limited period only. Around about 1895, a sign announcing the building was for sale appeared on the land, and the California Silk Culture Association closed its doors forever.

Some years later Mr. C. A. Hooper, of San Francisco lumber fame, purchased the abandoned property. He ordered the old, unsightly structure demolished and soon erected on a more desirable location a new home. Mrs. Hooper, mother of Mrs. Wigginton R. Creed, has since occupied this beautiful estate at the end of Mountain Avenue. Moreover, the elderly Mr. Ewer did not wish to leave Piedmont, so he selected a lot on Vernal Avenue and built a roomy cottage. In recent years this home was wrecked to make room for the new Safeway Store. Over this property, which includes the corner, there have been many years of litigation regarding zoning for business purposes.

But previous to this and after Ewer's death the house came into the ownership of a retired coffee dealer from South America and his family, the Berkenfelds. They lived here for quite a length of time while the two sons, Paul and John, grew up. John and his wife, with his son and elderly mother still reside in Piedmont on Bonita Avenue.

The Wetmore and Sherman Properties ...

Although the Spring grounds were sadly neglected after the Hotel fire, the surrounding acreages developed into a most desirable district for those who were content with the hourly horse-car service and other inconveniences of suburban living. Martin Miller and the horses did not work after six-thirty in the evening. This rural existence appealed so strongly to Jesse L. Wetmore that he gave his Tenth Street property in Oakland to his daughter and son-in-law, Dr. George Edwin Sherman, and bought for himself, his wife and two unmarried daughters a piece of land between Vista and Magnolia, facing Bonita Avenue. On each corner he constructed a large square bungalow, with wide verandahs surrounding three sides. Mr. and Mrs. Wetmore lived on the Vista Avenue corner (that house still stands).

The Magnolia Avenue cottage became the residence of Mrs. Sherman, now a widow, with her sons, Edward, John, George, and daughter Vida. All were our early schoolmates. The senior Wetmores were frequently visited by the son, Clarence, whose fame for his Cresta Blanca wines has spread far and wide. The vintage was produced from his delicately flavored grapes grown in the Livermore Valley and is now difficult to surpass.

This Wetmore property will appear several times again in the succeeding pages, as the house on the Magnolia corner has sheltered families whose names have been outstanding in Piedmont annals.

First Dairy in the City ...

Before leaving this corner, it might be interesting to note that in the early years of the twentieth century the broad-roofed bungalow (now the First Church of Christ, Scientist) was occupied by Mrs. Nellie Maxwell-Osborne, sister of Mrs. Frank Havens. In time this resourceful lady acquired some acreage in Jack Hayes Canyon, just above the cemetery boundary line. Here she ran the first dairy farm that supplied milk to the Piedmontese. It was known as Maxwelton Brae, and behind its gates were gathered in friendly pasture all the outmoded family cows, with the well-known Mr. Bauber as their keeper.

Soon a horse-drawn wagon made its daily round to kitchen doors, and from the heavy ten-gallon cans Mr. Bauber would pour fresh bubbling milk into waiting receptacles. Today a smartly styled delivery truck with THISTLE CREAMERY emblazoned on its sides, climbs about the circuitous roads with the same genial driver delivering his products to the children and grandchildren of his early customers.

A Gala Party for Amy Requa ...

As the eighties came to a close, great advertising schemes were being developed in San Francisco and in Oakland by those who had tracts of land for subdivisions, and the effect of this stir reached even to these quiet hills. However, Piedmont became more distinctly publicized through the many distinguished guests who were entertained by Mr. and Mrs. Requa. Others also felt the charm of the countryside; these included those who come from far and near to enjoy the driving and superb views.

For the most part, residents were content to leave these peaceful hillsides in the brilliant colorings of nature before man carved out the new roadways and measured lots. Following this pattern, the people participated enthusiastically in the varied activities of a quiet country life.

Diversions came, however, that were far from rural and simple. One party especially stands out in my mind as the epitome of the opulent style set by this leading family. Honoring her little daughter Amy, Mrs. Requa sent out invitations for a luncheon gathering of her children's friends at the end of July in 1886. When I received mine, preparations were commenced at once. From Taft and Pennoyer's Store on Broadway, Mother selected a lovely yardage of fine white embroidery, which the seamstress made up into a dress for the occasion. A wide silk blue sash, tied in a huge bow in the back, completed the

First Piedmont School—1891

festive attire. Matching loops of ribbon were tied about my two long braids of brown hair.

Ready for the party at last, a timid little girl climbed into the family carriage to be driven over to the Highlands by the hired man, and accompanied by the second girl as chaperone (our feminine help was called "girl", not "maid", in our household). Upon entering the gateway of the Requa estate, the various equipages formed a long queue on the asphalt drives as they curved through the formal green lawns dotted with an occasional clump of waving pampas grass.

Slowly the carriage approached the imposing front steps of the mansion. Here the little guests were met by attendants who shepherded them up the wide double doors. George Washington, the butler, led them into the great house. What a gathering! Of course, many were friends of the hostess from Field's Seminary, and the swains were from Hopkins Academy, then the fashionable private school for boys in Oakland. These and others were the future beaux and belles of San Francisco and Oakland. Some may have even come from New York for this party, or may have been passing through San Francisco at the time. The beautiful and vivacious Birdie Fair often visited at the Highlands.

Faint Line Between Fairyland and Reality . . .

Recalling the memories of this elaborate occasion, I see long tables at which the youthful guests were seated and where luncheon was served. At one place stood a gorgeous white cake, towering to an unbelievable height and trimmed with sparkling decorations. This was Amy's birthday cake. With the gay throng refreshed, the fond mothers ushered us into the double parlors, where chairs had been arranged and at one end there hung curtains concealing a raised platform.

Entertainment then followed, and the young groups took part enthusiastically. Everything seemed so tastefully arranged by the many sophisticated "mammas" of the day. Chiefly do I recall the mistress of ceremonies, Mrs. Phelps, from New York, the eldest daughter of the L. A. Booths. She was visiting at Hazelwood at this period, next to the Requa property.

The outstanding feature of this delightful party came when a series of Mother Goose tableaux were enacted. Actors were chosen from the audience, with each little guest having a turn. It was thrilling to be posed as one of the "silver bells among the cockle shells" in "Mary,

Mary, Quite Contrary". It was difficult to keep my head still while the fairy went tip-toeing around with her wand and sprinkling can.

This was certainly a party in keeping with the California fortunes which followed the gold rush days and the advent of the transcontinental railroads.

The Richardson Family ...

The name of Richardson, now perpetuated in the annals of our city, appears on the local records during 1889. A young couple, then living down in the Piedmont Avenue district, considered the hills ideal for a home and quickly purchased four acres along Mountain Avenue, just opposite the Wing estate. Two acres of this property were sold to Dr. Buckle who later built the much famed log cabin. On their own portion Mr. and Mrs. Richardson erected a comfortable home and along with their children, Charlotte and Girard, moved up in the Fall of 1890.

After constructing a fence about their small estate, the couple then planned and laid out a garden, the winding path leading to the latticed framework of a grape arbor. Here, when the ripe fruit hung in profusion, Mrs. Richardson entertained at simple afternoon gatherings. The aroma of freshly squeezed juice and a basketful of homemade cookies inspired her friends to action on the numerous causes for which she was constantly striving.

The first publications of the *Piedmont Weekly News* were edited by Mrs. Richardson, and she served in that capacity during the years of its sponsorship by the Church Women's Guild. Her keen, reportorial eye and rare ability as a writer made her articles of great import and interest. On Sunday, December 10, 1922, memorial services were held at the Piedmont Interdenominational Church for Mrs. J. B. Richardson. A beloved citizen had departed from our midst.

Sewell P. Channel and the Divining Rod ...

Only a few families during the late eighties and early nineties were brave and courageous enough to surmount the innumerable difficulties of home building high in the Piedmont district. Water was of greatest importance and had assumed a place out of all proportion to itself because only a limited supply was available and that at a prohibitive cost.

Aside from the simple Lawrence home on Vernal Avenue, there were open fields, green or brown according to the season, between the two blocks towards the west. These remained empty until Mr. Sewell P. Channel, a retired lumber magnate from Minneapolis, arrived on this coast in 1889. He and his wife, with their two young daughters Bessie and Mabel, were eager to find a permanent homesite. After careful and thoughtful consideration Mr. and Mrs. Channel decided to establish themselves in Piedmont. They purchased one half of that block of land bounded by Bonita to the east and Vista to the south. The unpaved roadway to the west was christened Hillside Avenue by this enterprising gentleman.

After selecting this property with its commanding view over Oakland and directly opposite the Golden Gate, Mr. Channel proceeded to erect the mansion which in later years became the home of Henry Butters of South African fame and was purchased from him by the Sisters of the Holy Family to be used as a convent.

Mr. Channel had the wild fields laid out into lawns encircled by gardens of exquisite taste and beauty. He also maintained a well-filled stable and carriages. The cordiality and kindness of these new neighbors made welcome additions to our community. The problem of a private water supply had evidently been considered in the planning of the estate, for previous to the beginning of construction, Mr. Channel had supervised the digging of a personally located well on his property. A windmill and tank were erected, making this new innovation a topic of keen interest and discussion to those who were paying the atrocious price of one dollar per thousand gallons for water, while here, seemingly out of nowhere came an abundant supply.

How was this "liquid gold" to be discovered elsewhere? "By the witch-hazel crotch," Mr. Channel stated simply. These were certainly easily obtainable, as the gulches were filled with hazel nut bushes. He emphasized that the hazel crotch had to be of a proper size and cut fresh during the season while the sap was still running.

With the water question assuming such vital importance, especially in the Craig family, our new neighbor offered to make his experiment on our property. At the appointed hour Mr. Channel commenced his pacing across and over various portions of the orchard and fields with the branches of the crotch held in a firm grip within both his hands. Watching him with conflicting emotions of curiosity and fascination were my father and mother, myself and several skeptical onlookers, waiting expectantly for the miracle to occur. A section thought to be most suitable for a well was suggested, on a high spot among some fruit trees. Soon, to our amazement, the point of the crotch began to dip down towards the earth. To the wonder of all this happened again and again. Mr. Channel kept criss-crossing the line of pull until the most desirable location had been chosen.

Magic Crotch Much in Demand . . .

There came such a strong pull on the fresh piece of hazel wood that it required the combined strength of Channel's two powerful hands to hold it in a horizontal position. Others then experimented with the magic crotch but had absolutely no response. It seemed as though something preternatural had happened before our incredulous eyes. Mr. Channel apparently possessed a magnetic attraction to an unusual degree.

With the courage and faith that characterized my father he immediately engaged a well-boring outfit. After three feet of excavation in a circle of five feet in diameter the diggers came to hard sandstone and not long afterwards to hard blue basalt rock. No one could predict the depth the digging might have to go before striking the stream of underground water. Having previously sunk much money in a Nevada gold mine, Father was acquainted with some real miners who were idle at this time. He sent for them, and they were put to work at cutting, blasting, and excavating a deep shaft.

Meantime, interest hereabouts grew keen, and at the end of each day when the miners were being hauled up to the surface by the windlass, an assembled group of persons were eagerly awaiting the report that water had at long last been struck. But the good news was long delayed, and many twenty dollar gold pieces were brought over from California Street for the Saturday pay-rolls. Sometimes Monday would dawn with a short-handed crew, since recovery from periodical sprees over the weekend required an extra day or two to recover. But indomitable faith in that witching rod stimulated an interest to continue the work. Seventy-two feet they went down before they were rewarded by a trickling stream. This created a real cause for joy and celebration. Mr. Channel beamed with happiness, as did Captain Lawrence and all the other neighbors who had been close and constant observers.

Then new problems appeared and had to be surmounted. As more blasting of the giant powder opened new fissures in the basalt rock, the flow of water kept increasing. A pump had to be installed when

Father ordered the well be made eight feet deeper and, if possible, of a wider diameter. An eighty foot well was finally completed, the water level rising to eighteen feet. A windmill and a 10,000 gallon tank were then installed, the latter built on a high and heavy timbered scaffolding.

The fact of a generous water supply gave a wonderful sense of security to the entire family, and our lawns were consequently kept greener and the garden extended. But even then came periods of trouble. During some years the mild summer breezes were too gentle to turn the heavy windmill. At this time Father would anxiously scan the pointer on the twelve-foot tank gauge upon his arrival home from San Francisco. Despite our abundant water supply, wind was an essential prerequisite, and this gift from nature did not await the bidding of man, nor was it induced by the waving of a twig of a witching rod. Expenses seemed never-ending. The lack of wind meant the installation of a horse-power pump and thus added to the duties of our burdened but dignified dapple gray carriage horse. Rather disgustedly, he adapted himself when blindfolded to the humiliating task of pulling the windlass around and around in never ending circles.

This underground experiment in the very heart of Piedomnt definitely established the fact that the entire locality had under it a hard rock foundation of great firmness. Conclusive proof of this fact came at the time of the 1906 earthquake, when chimneys stood firm and damage was practically nil.

Several other wells were later located by Mr. Channel, among them that of the Richardsons'. Like others in the vicinity, this family found the water supply wholly inadequate. After the Craig well had demonstrated the continuous flow of water, the Richardsons invited Mr. Channel and his divining rod to locate for them an underground stream also. With another miracle accomplished there soon arose at the rear of the property a tank and twirling windmill, pumping gallons whenever the amicable breezes blew.

FOURTH PERIOD—1890-1907

Steady Growth of the Community . . .

At the dawning of those happy years known across the land as the "gay nineties", the charm of this *Piedmonte* of California became recognized throughout the local communities and was heralded to the many distinguished visitors arriving in the city across the Bay.

For years the Requa family mansion atop the heights was the distinctive and identifying feature of this suburb. To this gracious and hospitable home came the elite of Oakland, while fashionable carriages and hacks also brought visitors from New York, among them the great railroad magnates and their ladies, with whom Mr. and Mrs. Requa had close association and friendship.

The crisp, bracing winds from the Pacific brought fleets of sailing ships from Europe and the Orient to the metropolis by the Golden Gate. Great fields of yellow poppies and blue lupines blazed on these green hillsides across the Bay. From almost every viewpoint the Mount Tamalpais Ridge loomed against the western skies, partially separating the Bay from the Pacific Ocean. According to the ancient Indian legends, there lies upon Mount Tamalpais a sleeping maiden who for centuries has awaited the awakening kiss of her lover.

With the rapidly increasing population the problem of transportation was a subject of importance to everyone. Only by improved service could outlying tracts of land be developed and made available for new homes. As San Francisco was emerging from the days of the horse-drawn cars, so Oakland and its suburbs felt the need of more modern means of conveyance. The sanddunes and cobblestones over the steep hills of the peninsular city had been cruel taskmasters to the faithful steeds that drew the heavy cars.

Before enlarging upon the building of the cable road along the newly surveyed steep grades to Piedmont, it may be well to obtain a glimpse at the historic ventures which were transforming our neighbor across the Bay into a cosmopolitan and commercial center.

The Dreamer That Created Reality ...

San Francisco had experienced the periods of depression, panic and booms, and these conditions were similarly reflected throughout the adjacent cities and towns. A mining panic occurred in August, 1873, sweeping away the life savings of many and accumulated fortunes for others. Then ensued one of the blackest periods in the history of California. Into this scene stepped a dreamer, not of a gold empire but of a street railway without visible motive power: passenger cars drawn by an underground cable to conquer the hills in a route to a new subdivision; mechanical cars to replace the ancient horse-drawn cars. Even in the East and in Europe there was no such innovation. Unheeding and grimly determined, Andrew Hallidie perfected the mechanical details that made his dream into a reality.

In such a setting the ground work was laid for the first cable system in America; the idea came to Mr. Hallidie during an accident in the winter of 1869. One evening he had paused to watch an overloaded streetcar start up one of the steep hills. A cold rain had been falling all day, and impatient men and women with taut nerves had crowded the little car until there did not seem enough room even for the proverbial "one more".

Slowly and with the utmost difficulty the four horses had managed to get the car in motion. When half a block had been covered, one horse slipped on the smooth cobblestones. The driver instantly applied the brakes, but he applied so much force and so suddenly that he snapped the chain. The car at once began to slide backwards down the hill, dragging the bodies of the poor, unfortunate horses over the stones, until the vehicle had reached the level of a cross street where it was stopped. As Hallidie assisted in releasing the mutilated animals, he resolved to work out a means of making such accidents impossible.

So the first cable was planned in San Francisco in 1871 and constructed upon the Clay Street hills soon thereafter. The indefatigable Andrew Hallidie perfected the mechanical details that made his dream a reality. It is easy to visualize the pride of San Franciscans in this new mode of transportation. People from far and near came for a ride on those cars with their intriguing mode of traction hidden underground.

Cable lines became easily the chief topic of conversation among the gentlemen with the high silk toppers as they commuted on the ferry boats from their East Bay homes to do business on California Street, then the financial hub of San Francisco.

Cable Car Fever Contagious ...

As early as 1882 a cable road in Chicago had been installed with apparently great success. Philadelphia followed suit a year later, and New York in 1886. By that time the East Bay was caught in the spreading vogue for this mechanically powered mode of travel. In 1883 a "Broadway Cable Railroad Company" was incorporated to build a line from Temescal to Fourteenth Street. Following the lapse of this project, the Oakland Railroad Company, while under the management of James G. Fair, in 1886 installed a cable system from the foot of Broadway, north to San Pablo Avenue, and continuing north on San Pablo to Emeryville. Several years later, the Blair-Howe interests ex-

Looking East over the Crocker Tract—1880 or 1884

panded. They had already developed extensive horse-car lines under the title of the Broadway and Piedmont Railway Company. Then the Fourteenth Street Railway Company (Blair's) began converting the Piedmont lines to cable railways. In 1887 they incorporated the Broadway, Berkeley and Piedmont Railway Companies with authorized capital stock of $500,000 to build lines aggregating eight miles in length. They also acquired the properties of the Broadway and Piedmont Railway Company (Blair's), which was accomplished through the exchange of $100,000 in stock, but shortly thereafter Walter Blair died and the project languished.

Before the next company was formed, however, serious attempts were made by its promoters to secure subsidies of $100.00 per acre from land-holders who would profit by it. This is about the date that Heron and Holcomb, the realtors, began acquiring Vernon Heights and Linda Vista tracts of unimproved lands, and it was through these sections that the planners of the projected cable line directed their surveys, rather than out Piedmont Avenue way. After the preliminary surveys had been completed and an entirely new artery created, they named it Oakland Avenue.

Expenses Mount Higher Than Anticipated . . .

According to some old reports, it is said that the costs mounted to eighty thousand dollars per mile over this new route, which was almost twice the sum originally contemplated. The entire car-lines of the Blair-Howe interests had been absorbed by this new company and their stock holdings greatly inflated. When during the later years the stock became heavily assessed, these men had to default. The many acres of land held by Mr. Howe and Mr. Blair, out Piedmont Avenue and up to Vernal Avenue, were thus deprived of the expected development for the horse-cars discontinued service when the cable arrived. "So the Howes went broke and the Blair estate was irretrievably involved in the cable venture." (1)

But the stage was set now for the coming boom in home building over the virgin fields of green grass and wild flowers.

While the aging, weary teams were still pulling their ever increasing loads of tourists up through the hay fields to the sulphur Springs the surveys were completed and the trench digging begun on the much heralded cable road to Piedmont.

---

(1) *Oakland Enquirer*, August 1, 1901.

New Neighbors Come with the Cable Line ...

As this tremendous new enterprise took shape, William A. Aldrich, president of the San Francisco Tool Company, purchased the block of land with home at Blair and Hardwick Avenues. This had been built for the Wright family and was a large, square dwelling with fine hardwoods used as the interior finishings. There were also the stable and cow barns and all the other appurtenances that are required on a small farm. Changes were made in the original house to adapt it to the needs of the delightful Bartons with their small sons, Aldrich and Willard, Mrs. Barton presided as hostess for her younger sister and for her father. Her sister, always gay and full of fun was Piedmont's first bride when she became Mrs. George P. Dunning.

The San Francisco Tool Company was furnishing all of the steel equipment and the wire cable for the new line. Presumably, Mr. Aldrich considered it wise to live in the vicinity, where he could keep an eye on the progress of the stupendous job ahead.

Soon trench digging and track laying commenced at Seventh and Broadway, straight out to Twenty-Fourth Street, thence turning east, where it circled on two sides the beautiful homesite of the James Moffitts. Their entire block was laid out in lawns and gardens with tall, majestic trees hiding the house from the passersby. It was one of the outstanding estates in Oakland, and the family within formed a nucleus for social life and gaiety. Later this was carried to Piedmont by Mr. James K. Moffitt and family who entertained in their lovely home amidst its garden setting.

Two Cables Necessary for the Journey ...

When the cable had traversed Twenty-Fourth Street, it turned eastward for two blocks, then turned again onto Harrison Street, and north once more at Twenty-Fifth Street. Here the brick powerhouse with all its engines and huge wheels was being built. The boys used to like nothing better than to stand watching that complicated machinery in motion. This location was at the start of the pull, and, if memory serves correctly, there were two cables: one for the hill section and another for the level portion of the road. At this point, the survey commenced on the grading for the artery, formerly Piedmont Avenue and henceforth to be known as Oakland Avenue. The right-of-way climbed up, dipped down, then up once more, cutting through virgin fields of native grass to the heights, known at this time as Linda Vista

Terrace. From there the road dipped down again, crossing a deep ravine over which the cars were carried on a high wooden trestle almost into Pleasant Valley. From there the climb continued up a series of steep grades, over cuts and fills, until it reached the topmost Avenue, then known as Vernal but now called Highland. At this intersection a turntable was installed and was raised a few feet above street level.

It was an intriguing pastime to watch the shining new cars land on that delicately balanced circle, with its rim of steel moving so easily within the protective base of concrete fortified with metal.

Activity at the Turntable ...

The conductor would hop off and push the car around until it joined the tracks for the downhill run. However, this was not the regular procedure; usually only a half turn to the single track on Vernal Avenue was made. Here the motorman lifted the "grip" and slowly the heavy car gained momentum along the Avenue to Moraga Road, where passengers would often alight to enjoy the attractions in the wooded ravine known as Blair Park. The fancy entrance had its turn-stile, which twirled around as an attendant seized a ticket from the eager entrant.

This spot became recognized as the end of the line. From here the cars could again obtain momentum for that most thrilling ride through the grain fields on the "gravity curve trolley". Connections were again made at Oakland Avenue, at a point near Carmel Avenue. There the heavy grip picked up its wire cable and proceeded with proper decorum down into the city. That little spurt of free speed, curved among the fields, was always a gay, abandoned ride, the degree depending upon the daring of the gripman and the hilarity of his passengers.

The construction of this road was quite an undertaking for those days. After the surveys were completed, deep cuts had to be blazed with intervening fills and trestles. Then came the horses dragging the huge plows to open a trench for the forming in concrete of the cable slot. Hundreds of laborers were employed, and a great amount of heavy hauling had to be pulled over poorly paved roads.

Frequently, after school hours and during that summer of 1890, our ponies trotted us over the newly constructed grades, hitherto inaccessible to traffic. Mounted on a side-saddle and costumed modishly in the long skirted riding habit of the day, we behaved with great dignity, despite the fact that much of it was enforced by the length of the trailing material that covered even the ankle and foot in the stirrup.

Observations on these jaunts were often rewarded by the sight of perhaps ten to twelve heavy dray horses straining in their every sinew to haul a huge load up over soft, dusty roads to some designated location.

Cable Line Stimulates Interest in Piedmont ...

The advent of this most modern invention naturally stimulated the interest and eagerness among those families who lived such a distance from their contemporaries in Oakland. The ancient horse-drawn cars were far too slow for all practical purposes, and those faithful beasts that had long drawn their master's carriages seemed loathe to demean themselves by stepping into their best trotting form for those five miles down to Taft and Pennoyer's Dry Goods Store or to Rice and White's Butcher Shop at Twelfth and Washington Streets. These pet horses had acquired much intelligence, and one knew just how much they dreaded that long, hard pull on the return to their barn and barley.

Opportunists Arrive with the Cable ...

No sooner was the cable line completed than suddenly there appeared opposite the turntable at Oakland and Vernal Avenues a large sign that read, "William J. Dingee, Real Estate." This shrewd businessman displayed tremendous foresightedness. Previously he had bought up the large tract of land between the Blair property on the north and the Craig estate on the south, and the eucalyptus forest as its eastern boundary. Through the center of this property he carved the final extension of Oakland Avenue, thus making available a great number of lots for home-sites.

The records show that in 1894 W. J. Dingee, A. H. Breed and Company, along with a few others, began to collect a fund for the express purpose of advertising Oakland and its surrounding countryside, publishing and distributing pamphlets and data concerning the desirability of this city and its suburbs for homes and business locations. This inaugurated a period of real development on the Dingee tract in Piedmont.

Then, after much fanfare, came a culminating and colorful event, rivalling even the Sunday balloon ascensions at Blair Park. An auction was scheduled for a certain Saturday. Many signs were placed along the route and flags and bunting were attached to trees and promised fun and refreshments at the appointed time and place. Then new lumber was brought and a platform was constructed close to the Craig fence. From this vantage point the auctioneer could shout tempting descriptions of his land divisions and the customary bargaining that goes on at an auction. Behind him were seats for the uniformed members of a brass band. Alternately each took turns at keeping the prospective buyers happy and tried to maintain the jovial, holiday atmosphere. An extra audience of round-eyed boys and girls were sitting rather precariously on the slanting top rail of the fence just behind the bandstand. This was certainly an afternoon to remember in our quiet, country lives. Sandwiches and pink lemonade were freely dispensed to everyone present.

It might seem superfluous to mention that the lots were soon disposed of, deposits were laid down and speculation became rife: a boom was predicted with many new homes prophesied in the immediate future.

Harsh Realities Hit the Prophets ...

However, the bubble burst and the building pace slowed down. Soon numerous sales on that first gala day turned into sad losses for the over-exuberant speculators, and the lots reverted to the persons or to the banks from whom the money was borrowed.

A slight depression overshadowed any marked progress during the next few years. Even the stimulus of the cable line and the Blair Park attractions brought only picnickers and transient crowds.

But new and revolutionary ideas were in the air. The marvelous power obtainable through electric current was lauded. This power had already been applied to the traction of cars on level roads, but now it was soon to be tried out on a Moraga hill. If the experiment proved successful, it would attract to these quiet hillsides visitors of both local and international fame, and with them might be ushered in another era of prosperity.

Piedmont Cable Company Suffers Losses ...

Financially, the Piedmont Cable Company became deeply involved and was forced into receivership in the October, 1893, when interest on its bonds was defaulted. A bond holders' committee was then formed, constituted of C. R. Bishop, S. C. Bigelow, Henry Rogers, J. R. Spring and H. S. King. The Court appointed Ira Bishop as receiver. For several years the directors of the Consolidated Piedmont

Horse Car in front of St. Mary's College—1889

Cable Company had recognized that electric railways might prove preferable to cable systems.

These properties were operated by the receiver, until they were sold at a foreclosure, March 19, 1895. At the sale they were bought by the bond holders' committee for sixty-two thousand dollars and were conveyed to the Piedmont and Mountain View Railway Company, April 1, 1895.

The money was borrowed from the Oakland Bank of Savings, and the new company assumed it. Prior to receivership, the company had purchased electric railway cars, dynamos, and the rest of the equipment, except for the poles and overhead wire. It was estimated by the receiver that switch-over would reduce operating expenses by fourteen thousand, six hundred dollars a year.

Experimental Tracks for Electric Railroad Laid . . .

The tentative track for the testing of the electric power pull was installed on the south side of Moraga below Vernal, because this portion was particularly steep. Electric current had been brought up to Blair Park, making it comparatively simple to have the wires connected with this temporary line across the street. So here the first experiments for testing the practical use of an over-head trolley in the East Bay took place.

A specially equipped car was hauled up from the power-house and then was switched over to the temporary track. Great interest centered around this invention, and the watching people were fascinated as they saw the heavy loads pulled up the grade by the newly discovered "magic power". The success of this venture seemed to portend a coming era of prosperity, for soon the once-famed cable cars were discarded and the continuous rumble of the heavy wire cable over the small wheels down in the slot were no longer heard.

The new green electric cars ran for a time, but in a few years the route over the cable tracks which they had been using was abandoned, after a new survey had brought the line out along Piedmont Avenue until it reached Mather Street at the old Junction. There the tracks turned eastward through cuts and fills and over the same rolling fields where once had crawled the outmoded horse-cars. Surveyors and road graders soon transformed the old Blair tract into salable homesites, where yet another section of the coming city of Piedmont was developed.

The Widely Traveled Butters Family . . .

California, still young in its own history, has gathered within its borders men and women from many distant lands. Their intrepid courage and wide intelligence have contributed to the historic splendor that belonged to this period. For example, two young men from New England, Charles and Henry A. Butters, came from South African mines and settled here. Some lives seem ruled by the spirit of adventure, and these brothers were destined to live out their lives dramatically in high places throughout the world. They were tops in the field of sports and possessed remarkable business acumen. Charles became a mining engineer in the Transvaal Republic and amassed a fortune also out of the gold mines of Johannesburg. Henry, his youngest brother, made great wealth through trade along the diamond deposits from Kimberly to Cape Town.

The call of home brought Mr. and Mrs. Charles Butters back to America, but his tall, good-looking bachelor brother went to London, instead, where many of his South African friends and associates were located, enjoying the constant whirl of new diversions and pleasures. The restless spirit of his dynamic family characteristics soon induced him to follow his brother to California, where he met and married a gracious widow who had a brood of equally lovely children.

This couple lived for a while in San Francisco, and in April, 1892, a baby was born to them, the son and heir to a very great fortune. A drama worth recording came to Piedmont through Henry A. Butters, who bought their great turreted, mid-Victorian house at Hillside and Vista Avenues. This entire block had recently been transferred by the Channels to Len Houghton who, in turn, sold the improved half to the Butters. Immediately after the purchase was completed, contractors proceeded to enlarge and repaint the entire interior and exterior of the house, in preparation for the gaiety soon to re-echo from its walls. It was appropriately named Alta Vista, as from that height an unobstructed view stretched out toward the blue waters of Lake Merritt.

Butters Family Adds More Glow to Piedmont . . .

So in the Spring of 1896, little Harry was brought by his doting parents to the big yellow house which was surrounded by bright flowers and wide lawns, bordered by graceful palms. Its low steps and wide verandahs offered a generous welcome to guests.

The mother in this household possessed a warm-hearted generosity and hospitality, radiating her innate love and peace to all about her. Wealth provided the gratification of all temporal desires. Fine horses and carriages filled the stables; whenever the pealing notes of the hunter's horn sounded, the eager youth of Piedmont ran to Vernal Avenue to catch a fleeting glimpse of the brightly painted tally-ho as it dashed by. Mr. Butters always handled the reins and plied the whip when necessary, driving his sleek four-in-hand as he did in England. A liveried coachman sat by his side ready for any emergency and to assist the ladies to and from their high seats.

In the basement ballroom the great house provided the setting for dances and the amateur theatricals, then the vogue of the day. The *Oakland Tribune* of January 17, 1905, carries an announcement customary in that era: "Mrs. Henry Butters and Miss Butters are at home on Wednesday during January, and their Piedmont home will be the scene of an informal gathering tomorrow." Some time later a large and brilliant reception was given in honor of a few visitors from abroad.

While the older children by Mrs. Butter's first marriage enjoyed every advantage which social position offered, they gave to their younger half-brother the deepest affection and devotion. He was most carefully schooled and protected, and one recalls that even on his daily canters across the hills on his pony Billy he was always accompanied by a groom.

For a few years Harry attended the local Piedmont public school. But on one of the trips to Europe Mr. and Mrs. Butters took the young lad with them, and, as he was then fourteen, they decided to enroll him at Beaumont College, otherwise known as Old Windsor. There he learned the true meaning of England and his valuable English heritage. The devotion that was conceived in those early years played a major role in his final decision which caused him to enter World War I, because he felt a real debt to that tradition.

The earthquake of April 18, 1906 which brought disaster to San Francisco had a tremendous repercussion on the fortunes of the communities in the Bay area and on those who had made great investments in their development. The elder Butters had put his heart and most of his resources into the Northern Electric Railway Line. His health broke under the strain, and his death came with stunning suddenness, October 26, 1908.

Tragedies Hit Young Harry ...

Harry had returned from England and had gone with his mother to Los Angeles, realizing beyond his years the nature of the clouds that rolled over his domestic horizon. At the news of his father's death the boy, who had returned to England for a few more years' study at Exeter, came home to Piedmont early in 1909. In the Spring of that year he had suffered an attack of pleurisy and spent his convalescent period at Yosemite with his mother. Here another tragedy befell the young man when his mother died in June in the splendid silence of the great valley, where she had fondly hoped that he would be restored to health. The boy himself drove the team which carried the precious burden to the railroad.

At the age of seventeen, his father's will had left Harry the heir to a large sum of the Butters' fortune, recently somewhat depleted, and now, to his great dismay, he discovered that he was the sole legatee to his mother's portion as well. After the reading of the second Will, there came a dramatic moment in the big study of Alta Vista. Harry quickly stood up, but he looked as though his years were forty-seven rather than seventeen, and announced quietly but firmly that he was forced to contest the Will. He stated flatly that his mother's estate must be equally divided among her eight children. His request became law.

Harry Comes Into His Majority ...

In April, 1913, Harry Butters became of age and assumed the management of his estate. He built a small bachelor's establishment for his own use on a corner of the Piedmont property, leaving a tall hedge that separated it from Alta Vista. This retreat, named the Igloo, adjoined the homes of the David Edwards and Lucile Bray.

A short period of happiness followed. He drove a spectacular automobile at top speed and was well known as a dashing player on the San Mateo polo grounds. Then, after this brief spurt of care-free living, came August 28, 1914. For Harry there was only one choice to make and that was to fight for England. Promptly he enlisted and started East on October 4, 1914. He looked so fit and alive that his friends saw him off with no shadow of foreboding crossing their minds or darkening their good wishes.

World War I Leaves Mark on Piedmont ...

During the long summer of 1915 our California recruit became one of the million khaki-clad figures in England. In the March of that year he received his first commission with the Eleventh Royal Warwickshire Regiment, entering directly into the active service. "He was a warm-hearted, fearless young officer, as fine as American gentleman as ever crossed the Atlantic." But the brief flame of his life ended in the battle for the Somme, August 21, 1916. In his twenty-fifth year Harry Butters was killed by the same shell that killed his battery commander. He rates as no ordinary man, and his name is carved with those of the other brave youths upon the marble memorial plaque which honors them at the Piedmont Civic Center:

MEMORIAL TO PIEDMONT HEROES OF WORLD WAR ONE

> Egbert William Beach. (2)
> Henry Augustus Butters
> Otto Julius Carlsen
> Frank J. Field
> Thomas Edward Graves
> Carl Castlemaine Jones

William E. Sharon Inscribes His Name ...

But to revert back again into the late Nineteenth Century, soon after the advent of electric service to Piedmont, another name of distinction appeared on County maps, that of William E. Sharon. His deed was recorded as the seven acres of land located on the upper side of Mountain Avenue, bounded by the Wing property on the southeast and Dormidera Avenue along the western line. This Sharon was a nephew of Senator William Sharon of the Comstock Lode who played such an important part in the colorful days of early San Francisco and was the owner of the first Palace Hotel.

Springtime buttercups and poppies covered this very beautiful location when the engineers began laying out a graded road circling up to the topmost level. Here preparations were commenced for the construction of a huge plastered house of semi-Spanish architecture. It was almost to rival the Requa house as an outstanding landmark.

---

(2) An East Bay school was named after Egbert William Beach.

Strange, that now, in the writing of these pages, the landscape, the house with its square-cornered turrets and the group that gave it such a life should come crowding back into consciousness with vivid clearness. The numerous members of this family of young people had overflowed the confines of the home at Nineteenth and Franklin Streets in Oakland. Light-hearted days were those when the horses and carriage brought these brothers and sisters to live on Sharon Avenue. For over twenty years they contributed greatly to the welfare and advancement of Piedmont. But now the big house is no longer there; it was wrecked to make way for many other residences of lesser dimensions.

William E. Sharon acquired varied interests in and about Virginia City, Nevada, where he married the vivacious Miss Mygatt. Here their elder children were born. He found it necessary, after moving to Piedmont to spend much time in the neighboring state, looking after business interests there. But when at home, all recognized him as a true gentleman, never too preoccupied to play with his children, romping with them in the games room on the third floor. Order and system, however, always prevailed in this well-run household, the details of which were supervised by the stately, tall and austere grandmother, Mrs. Mygatt. Her word or gesture merited prompt attention and obedience.

Formation of the Womens Exchange . . .

Mrs. Sharon, therefore, found time for charitable and social interests outside her home. She became the founder of the Women's Exchange, an institution of Oakland and patronized and supported by the "best people". The disbursement center had its location on Fourteenth Street between Washington and Clay. During the afternoon hours many fashionable carriages stopped before its doors, permitting the ladies to enter the attractive interior, where on one side were displayed delicious home-made cakes and pies. These delicacies were made by some of the best cooks in town, who took advantage of this opportunity to supplement their family incomes. Counters on the opposite side of the shop contained articles of the finest needlework. Names of many prominent Oakland women were on the Board of Directors and they helped to meet a need of the community. Mrs. Sharon served almost continuously as the president.

Active in Musical World . . .

As time went on she became more involved in the needs close about her own home. She expended much energy in the promotion of cultural gatherings and charitable benefits. However, this efficient mother found leisure to supervise and share in the social life of her growing family. Music, in its many facets, served as the center for most of the home entertainments.

On one occasion friends in Oakland and the scattered Piedmont neighbors received formal engraved invitations to a tea at the new home, the honor guest to be Madame Emma Nevada, a popular singer of the day. Her fame had begun during the boom years in Nevada, her native state, where they called her the sage-brush linnet. She later became a world-famous star.

This smiling prima donna, a gorgeously gowned blonde, with the generous curves of earlier days, greeted the guests as Mrs. Sharon presented them, before they moved on along the sparkling receiving line. The lovely young daughter, Florence Sharon, and her sister Blanche assisted their mother, aided by the two smaller girls, Ruth and Esther, all flitting about in new frilled party frocks. The three sons, Claude, Robert and Hurford, were at the entrance, escorting the guests to the door after the footman had helped them from their carriages. Fine young gentlemen were this trio of brothers in smart serge suits, knee pants, long black stockings and brightly shined shoes. And the younger boys wore wide turn-over collars with flowing bow ties of colored silk.

Strains of orchestral music greeted the guests as they entered the spacious central hall. The notes came floating out from behind a background of flowers and potted palms, thus giving a softening effect to the low hum of voices.

Luxuries of Wealth Artistically Arranged ...

The guests, wandering slowly from the double parlors across the hall to the dining room, were met by others of the receiving party. A long, artistically decorated table, sumptuous with its silver and cut glass, was laden with platters of delectable sandwiches and fancy cakes. The function seemed to savor of New York or London high society, especially when the maid inquired, "Do you wish rum in the tea?" When an affirmative reply was given, the hostess, pouring at the end of the long glittering table, added a few drops of this potent liquid from an exquisitely wrought jug at her right hand. Apparently this innovation was copied after a custom observed in the London drawing rooms of Lady Hesketh, daughter of Senator Sharon.

Cable Car at Blair Park

Cable Car at Oakland and Highland

Thus, before the turn of the century a Piedmont colony on the rise above Oakland had arrived socially, according to the society editors of Mr. Dargee's *Tribune* and those on the *Oakland Enquirer* staff. Most important of all, perhaps, was the weekly news sheet edited by Miss Mollie Connors, who loved life and people and the news of their activities. The eyes of many of Oakland's wealthier class were being focused for the first time on the hills, as they searched for future home sites.

Piedmont Weddings Between 1895-1904 ...

Before moving into the history of the new century a few weddings should be recorded. Mr. Mark Requa and Miss Florence Herrick were married at a formal ceremony in 1895 at the First Congregational Church of Oakland. Some years later Mark Requa brought his wife and children, Lawrence, Amy and the baby, to a large new home located up on Mountain Avenue. Alice Herrick, sister of Florence Requa, married Josiah Stanford. They planned a spacious, rambling home on Wildwood, just off Highland Avenue. Later Misses Lucy and Margaret Herrick built a home on Pacific Avenue.

Soon after the Mark Requa marriage, the daughter of the family, Amy Requa, became Mrs. Oscar Fitzallen Long at a brilliant ceremony at high noon in St. Paul's Church. A reception followed at the Highlands and distinguished guests were present from many parts of the country and even some from Europe.

Another event was to bring the host of Sharon connections and their friends together at St. Paul's Church. The eldest daughter Florence and Mr. Peter Allen were married at a lovely ceremony, after which the carriages drove the guests up to the new establishment for a gay aftermath.

Then on a cold, crisp evening a heavy closed hack, drawn by a pair of dapple grey horses, waited upon the gravel driveway at the Craig front steps to receive Louis William Pattiani and his bride, Evelyn Craig, on November 15, 1904. Our marriage was performed by Reverend Charles R. Brown at the family home and was immediately followed by a reception to our friends and neighbors.

Death of Isaac L. Requa ...

In sharp contrast with these festive occasions, sorrow and a sense of personal loss touched the hearts of friends and neighbors near to the Highlands, March, 1905. The death of Mr. Isaac L. Requa took from

Piedmont its outstanding citizen, a beloved and gracious gentleman, tall, dignified and handsome, always ready with a kindly word and smile. His death marked the close of an era, and portended the changes from rural estates with their extensive gardens to smaller subdivisions.

This change meant progress and helped to attract the increasing population as it moved up the grade from Oakland, envisioning a home on the hills for the younger generation. Many future inhabitants of Piedmont lived at that time on Madison, Alice, Oak, Brush and Castro Streets. From every walk of life they came: the artistic, wise and the discriminating beauty-lovers, all bent upon finding a California home of secure and endearing charm.

The earthquake of April 18, 1906, followed by the devastating San Francisco fire, caused a rapid influx of families to the East Bay, and with the great increase of homes Piedmont was soon to reach the envied status of a municipality.

Battle Over Free Educational Privileges . . .

The Oakland Board of Education had finally acceded to a long sought request by the citizens of the "Piedmont Sanitary District" to allow those children from that part of Alameda County who were eligible for the high school, to attend the Oakland High School without paying a special fee. My father had been active in advocating this adjustment in cooperation with other taxpayers who had been forced to pay twenty-five dollars each term to send their children to the high school at Twelfth and Market Streets in Oakland. I rode the cable cars to attend the "seat of learning" from 1891 to 1894, but Roy and Margery Craig were sent to private schools, which charged even higher tuition rates, in protest as Father was then agitating either for a local high school within the district or for the elimination of the extra fee. It caused some very heated arguments. However, records state that this section (meaning Piedmont). along with other schools, was annexed to "Oakland for school purposes only".

William J. Dingee and the Water Companies . . .

The progress of development in any community is always coincident with its water supply. During the early years immediately folowing 1900, the people of the entire East Bay were clamoring for better quality water and improved service.

When the old Contra Costa Company refused to purify the supply or reduce the price, the Oakland Water Company was organized by

William J. Dingee. This dynamic gentleman still lived on the estate at the head of Moraga Road, from whence he drove or rode his sleek horses over the hills to view with his own eyes the possibilities offered by natural depressions for water supply and conservation.

When the Dingee intentions became public, he was at first hailed as a public benefactor. He planned to secure the water not only from the Piedmont foothills but from the immense overflow of the artesian wells at Alvarado as well.

Great Popularity of the Scheme ...

Promptly the people rallied to his support. The rush of patronage was so great that the new company threatened to outstrip its rivals both in support and in public esteem. At once the rates were cut and the new company saved two hundred and fifty thousand dollars in Oakland alone. This reduction also proved a favorable inducement to those desiring homes in the Piedmont area.

Fortunately, the Oakland Water Company had come into operation just previous to several dry seasons when the Contra Costa lakes were down to their mud bottoms. Because of the lack of rain there was no grass, and cows and other livestock faced starvation. In an attempt to offset this danger, pipes were laid to Piedmont and to other high elevations from the lake near Claremont, which is 425 feet above the city, but this uncertain supply did not fulfill the demand.

Overtures and feelers went out to Dingee, and arrangements were finally consummated to have his Alvarado Wells connected with the Lake Chabot system. This forced merger produced hard water for the citizenry and a million dollars for Dingee.

With that fortune Mr. and Mrs. Dingee moved to San Francisco. He turned up next with a monopoly on the slate roof industry and followed that venture by obtaining control of the cement industry. He became an intimate of San Francisco's Mayor Eugene Schmitz. When the latter experienced his downfall, Mr. Dingee was the one who put up his two hundred thousand dollar bond. In 1908, however, the Dingee financial empire started to collapse, and shortly thereafter he retired to a modest house in Sacramento, where he died in 1941.

Fever of "Quick Wealth" Attacks the Country ...

The causes of certain events are frequently shrouded in mystery or more often, are purposely withheld from the reader. A true portrayal of a place and its people requires an understanding of the character

f the motivating forces which resulted in its growth. One can catch
he authentic color and spirit of a period when dealing with factors of
undamental significance, rather than with events of merely local
nterest.

A series of articles entitled "The Get Rich Quick Wallingfords",
published in *Harper's Magazine,* at about the turn of the century,
was typical of a condition where no law existed to protect the unsus-
pecting client. Across the country in every city and hamlet enterprising
promoters were fostering great schemes for abstracting the savings of
he public ready and eager to make money in the easiest way.

Many of these projects have proven in later years of commercial
advantage to the communities involved. Great benefit and pleasure
have been afforded to visitors and residents of the East Bay by the
vision of one man, translated into terms of active pursuits too numerous in this brief sketch to mention.

Frank C. Havens and the
Mutual Investment Company . . .

Frank C. Havens, son of Wickham Havens, a sea captain at Sag
Harbor, came to Oakland in the early nineties. He organized the Mutual Investment Company, assisted by salesmen who carried on a
rather questionable traffic throughout the state. After a few years this
scheme failed but a real estate holding company was formed with
offices in Oakland.

Mr. Havens then established a home for himself and his four sons,
Wickham, Harold (Bud), Saide and Paul, their mother having died
some years previously. She was the sister of Harmon Bell. The Havens
now lived in the Vernon Heights district. Later he was married to the
friendly and efficient Leila Rand, who from then on proved an able
helpmeet for him.

While a young man at Sag Harbor, he had studied landscape gardening, having by nature a taste for the aesthetic. So, in the gardens
surrounding his new home Mr. Havens developed fine varieties of
roses, which soon became famous for their rare beauty. There had
also arrived in Oakland from the same seaboard town a boyhood neighbor of the Havens, Francis Marion Smith, known as the "Borax King
of Death Valley". The two friends soon became closely allied in business ventures, for the wealth of the one could be used in financing
the new schemes with which the mind of the other was constantly
filled.

Organization of the Realty Syndicate ...

It is certainly true that Mr. Havens possessed the acumen of a promoter, unsurpassed in excellence, and gave great impetus to the growth and progress of Piedmont and the surrounding hills. He became the motivating force in the spending of millions accumulated by F. M. Smith. Together they organized the Realty Syndicate, obtaining control over some thirteen thousand acres within the East Bay region.

One project of great import, though not directly related to the Piedmont story, should be mentioned: the erection of the Claremont Hotel nestled in the western side of the Berkeley hills, a subject which could make a complete story in itself. In 1900 this tremendous hostelry of over 300 rooms was opened with a gay party for family and friends. Mr. Havens, assisted by architects and his efficient and talented secretary, Miss Mabel Nace, was the mind and force which planned a fitting place for the accomodation of visiting millionaires from eastern and European cities. He visioned a future for the Pacific Coast, perhaps a generation ahead of the actual achievement of his dream.

Throughout its first years the Claremont suffered many reverses. Success finally came during the latter part of the thirties, when it was taken over by Mr. and Mrs. Claude C. Gillum, the present owners. Improvements have been made throughout the structure, particularly the addition of a beautiful cocktail lounge overlooking the San Francisco Bay with its glistening waters in the day and the lights of the two bridges piercing the darkness of the night, and it is now one of the leading hotels in the United States.

Havens Changes Names of Piedmont Thoroughfares ...

While the Claremont Hotel was in the process of construction, the Havens interests were spreading over a wide area. Among his new projects was the development of the old and neglected Piedmont Springs Hotel property which he acquired at a very low figure from the hard-pressed owners who had surrendered their equities to the Oakland banks.

About this time the Sherman bungalow at Magnolia and Bonita Avenues became vacant, and Mr. Havens moved his family up from their Vernon Street home to this Piedmont corner. From this point he could better supervise the contemplated improvements soon to be made in and about the Sulphur Springs Canyon. As the Realty Syndicate holdings became more extensive, the promoters assumed an increasingly large influence in this central district.

Piedmont Springs Club House—1903

Several street names were soon changed on the later issue maps. Vernal Avenue, named years earlier by Walter Blair, was henceforth to be called Highland Avenue from Moraga to the gateway entrance of the Requa estate. Along its northern boundary ran Hazel Lane leading into the Booth property. From here the curving road on down to Lakeshore Avenue was signed as Buttercup Avenue and can be found under this title on all early maps. However, the new name of Wildwood was given to this colorful drive, and in the following years the glistening buttercups and poppies, like its old name, gradually disappeared from along the way.

Improvements on the Springs Grounds . . .

From 1907 through 1915, the Syndicate activities centered largely around the Springs grounds. The gardens were tended and beautified by the artistic hand of young Joseph Furtado. He supervised the company nursery, where he propagated tender eucalyptus trees, and a few years later he laid out their planting over the barren hills which Havens and the Syndicate had acquired. But Joe, as the neighbors called him, had also kept his men at work in the long neglected Spring canyon. Overgrown brush was removed and the walks widened on the incline along the stream which flowed into a large pool below. As the ground levelled and widened out, a natural amphitheatre was completed by using eucalyptus logs smoothed on one side for seats.

Amateurs of the day were soon performing their stunts down in this ravine. Their rude stage was opposite the grotto where out of a rock-walled cavern trickled two streams of sulphur water. One flowed through a fissure of pink-tinted rock, while the other squeezed its way between white-coated crevices. Various minerals are still present in those stony walls. A latticed house covered the top and sides of the cool cavern with its new cemented floors. Visitors found bright tin cups attached to long chains fastened at one end into the rocks close to the outlets.

A new generation was then coming to sample these waters: some made wry faces after the first sniff of sulphur, while others gulped it down for its medicinal virtues. The public were not then so destructive as to wreck this scene. They respected its charm and serene beauty.

While these grounds were being landscaped, Mr. Haven's architect, under the guidance of his personal assistant, Miss Mabel Nace, built the attractive Club House, directly opposite the present site of the shopping district.

In the clubhouse was installed a French chef, famed for his fine cuisine and ready to serve luncheon and dinner parties on order. The dining room and wide verandahs became popular with much of Oakland's *haut monde* and for the young people who came out for an evening of dinner dancing in "the good old summer time."

An artistic new fence ran along the Park frontage on Vernal Avenue, broken by a gateway and ticket office, and all entrants were hereafter required to pay a fee of twenty-five cents.

Formation of the Bohemian Club and Art Gallery . . .

The Syndicate directors spared no money in the improvement of their properties, which included the knoll now partially encircled by Guilford Road. Here under the supervision of experienced artists they built an art gallery of pretensious design and large floor space. To the south of this low, rambling building lay the recently vacated Randall estate at the Hazel Lane corner. Into this large, three-story house Mr. Havens now moved his family, leaving their Bonita and Magnolia bungalow. The larger home, when staffed with Oriental help, would afford greater opportunity for much entertaining, as the art gallery drew attendance from far and near.

Among the visitors came artists and young literary aspirants who frequented the Bohemian Club. George Sterling, Mr. Havens' nephew, often acted as host for "Uncle Frank", and, after viewing the paintings, these friends would be invited to enjoy the hospitality of the Haven's home. A welcome always awaited them in the big living room. Here they gathered about a log fire, sipping their drinks and discussing the problems of their various interests and talents.

Joaquin Miller and Jack London Among the Group . . .

Joaquin Miller drove over from his cottage near the head of Diamond Canyon, where he lived and wrote for many years. This home is now held by the City of Oakland as a shrine to the memory of the "poet of the Sierras". Herbert Whittier, the writer and poet who with his large family occupied the old Silk Culture house, was also one of the coterie. With him came Xavier Martinez, the artist, who married Elsie Whittier in 1907.

Jack London made his home for a few years on Worcester Heights in the cottage vacated by the Bowman family. His sturdy little mother occupied the smaller house, while he lived in the other cottage with his wife and two daughters. From this lofty eyrie, looking out through the Golden Gate, he gathered inspiration for some of his writings.

He, too, often joined these get-togethers, along with Albert Farr and other architects, the Partingtons, Arthur Putnam, Haig Pattigan and Roy Partridge. Both the latter helped to direct the purchase and arrangement of the very fine collection of art which adorned the gallery's circular rooms. Many of the paintings were accorded deserved recognition. Away from business, art became to these people a vital and growing reality, whether in painting, music or literature. It seems regrettable that such a promising enterprise could not have been preserved as a cultural center for Piedmont. At these convivial gatherings George Sterling could entertain for endless hours with his own verse. His first volume of poetry was published in 1903, but it was not until the publication of the *Wine of Wizardry* that he really achieved prominence.

Havens' Elaborate Plans for Mansion . . .

While the Havens were occupying the large house at the Hazel Lane corner, they selected as their permanent homesite an acreage of an oak-covered canyon across the road from the Highlands, giving it the appropriate title of Wildwood. Along its northern boundary at right angles to the newly named Highland Avenue came a shorter street which was mapped under the same name, and here an entrance way was opened into the new Wildwood gardens, where development now commenced.

Ideas and architects' plans for a most unusual house were taking form gradually within the family circle. When the plans were finally decided upon and formulated, workmen in great numbers soon had construction underway. Mrs. Leila Havens had long been a student of the Yogi religion. With the employment of professional people and the use of her own natural tastes and ability, a replica of an Oriental Rajah's dwelling was designed and built on this well chosen location.

It required over two years to complete the magnificent house and its superb interior finishings. Ship loads of pale teakwood hewn into huge beams and slabs were brought directly from India. At the same time several Hindu craftsmen came, too, and they spent almost three years in the cutting and carving of this wood for interior use. Two Japanese artisans were also kept busy, for it was truly a stupendous undertaking in our quiet countryside.

House Warming at Wildwood . . .

After all was completed and the family moved in, Mrs. Havens mailed out formal invitations to friends and neighbors for her house-warming. Everyone eagerly accepted, for the unique house had been much discussed. The hostess gaily greeted her guests as we entered the spacious reception hall and stepped onto the luxuriously padded floor of imported matting. It was almost as though we had been whisked off into a fantastic world of Aladdin and make-believe, as we lingeringly wandered about before descending the curved staircase leading to the floor below. Along its panelled side walls were carved niches and crevices in which reposed small Buddhas and rare Indian treasures. Upon arriving at the dining room entrance, our thoughts turned from Asiatic dreams to the beauty that appeared before us. The many round tables in the large octagonal room were gay with flowers, bright silver and sparkling crystal. Through the plate glass windows the outlook was southerly over a deeply wooded canyon with its ever-changing panorama of colors. A San Francisco caterer served a delicious repast to Mrs. Havens and her guests.

But the crowning thrill came after taking another stairway down its intriguing curves to the entertainment room on yet a third level. Floating up to us came the aroma of incense, and as we entered, the leaping flames from the logs in the great fireplace at the far end offered us a warm welcome. At the opposite end of that long room our gaze was attracted to another niche, this time large enough for the form of a s'anding life-sized Buddha. Then music began to sound, and from behind that thinly curtained statue appeared a dancing goddess, her lithe figure sheathed in a golden gown, topped off by an elaborate bejeweled headdress. To our astonishment we beheld in this dazzling creature the famous dancer Ruth St. Dennis. The glitter and dancing which followed held us enthralled, as we rested in that intimate setting surrounded by East Indian splendor and listening to the measured rhythm of the tom-tom music.

Friends of the Havens Family . . .

Soon after the completion of the Wildwood home and grounds, Mr. Havens gave attention to his late father's estate on Long Island. They remained back there only a short time. Before the outbreak of World War I in 1914 we can recall the Havens families, including those of Wickham and Harold, drawing about them others of various talents as well as many associated with the large financial ventures of this period. Mr. and Mrs. Norman de Vaux appeared at these gatherings and "Billy" Durant their partner in the automobile world. The de Vauxes decided to remain in this interesting suburb, so they built a large home on the Crocker tract in which they lived for many years. Since then it has been taken over by the genial Mr. and Mrs. C. R. Adams.

William C. Durant only hovered on the edge of this gifted circle of friends. He was much involved in bringing the General Motors Corporation into existence, for he held the controlling interest. However, after the World War slump he lost this control. He then played the stock market, in which he first made millions then finally lost everything in 1929. He died penniless in New York at the age of eighty-five. As a frequent visitor in Piedmont homes Billy Durant has been quoted as saying: "Money is only loaned to a man. He comes into the world with nothing and he leaves with nothing."

Failure of the Realty Syndicate ...

Facts of history record the achievements of people as they move through the allotted generations and then go off the scenes, while their contributions and creations live on for others to appraise.

During the years of World War I, the Realty Syndicate and Havens interests became financial failures. Visions of aesthetic beauty, followed by extravagant expenditures and consequent foreclosures, quite broke the strength of Mr. Havens, and when he died in 1918, he left an involved estate to his brave and capable widow, with no hope of possible recovery.

In their years of luxurious living and entertainment, she had presided over the Havens menage with dignity of bearing and warmth of friendship. Today the approach to many homes is made through the same gateway where at one time only those entering her private park drove to share in her famed hospitality. At one summer festival that I clearly recall Mrs. Havens permitted the grounds to be used for a baby hospital benefit. It was a fete after the fashion of those days which were formerly held in East Oakland on the beautiful estate of Mr. and Mrs. Francis M. Smith. Wildwood Gardens had aroused new interest in the annual event, and Society was eager to participate. Attractions were suited to all ages: booths of every description, pony rides, fortune telling, an evening supper, and dancing under the stars.

This affair was not open for public admittance, as tickets were obtainable only through private sources. Mrs. Anita Oliver Jensen, now Mrs. Lunn, worked most devotedly at these annual benefits, for the baby hospital had long been one of her "pet charities". Since she has moved from California, the presidency of various hospital branches has been most ably assumed by her sister-in-law, Mrs. Harold Oliver.

The Widow Carries on ...

Leila Rand Havens possessed an intelligence and demeanor that commanded affectionate regard from all her associates. The study of the Yogi religion and its philosophy afforded her much comfort and had become the motivating influence in her life. The later years for Mrs. Havens in that big, silent house found her in poor health and much alone. Her strength was overtaxed by the supervision of the huge estate that once included the Key Route Inn at Twenty-Second and Broadway Streets, the City's municipal water company, the Transit Company, and land stretching from San Leandro to Berkeley. After almost thirty years as mistress in Wildwood Gardens, the wearied spirit of the one who had inspired the erection of the East Indian replica departed from all her cares and responsibilities in June, 1932, during the Depression.

Short Duration of Piedmont Post Office ...

Returning again to these expanding and, apparently, prosperous years, Mr. and Mrs. Wickham Havens and sons Harold, Saide and Paul became very prominent in the life that centered about the Springs Club House. They did much toward continuing the music and entertainment there.

Piedmont by this time had attained a place of importance in and around the Bay area and felt that it was entitled to the distinction of having a Post Office of its own, to be located in the small square ticket house standing by the turn-stile entrance to the grounds. Mrs. Sharon and her coterie of guild workers managed to obtain an official rating for such a Post Office. Mrs. Mary Patton, already collector of the fee of admission, added to her duties the title and work of Postmistress.

The Federal Government made little or no appropriation to this venture, and Mrs. Patton was required to stamp a certain minimum of envelopes to carry a Post Office rating. With a rather meagre population and that scattered over a broad area, the men coming home from San Francisco helped swell the quota of out-going mail by dutifully carrying their bunches of business letters across the Bay to mail them at Mrs. Patton's cubicle. The flurry of neighborhood pride in running over there to get our mail lasted for only a few years. The United States flag disappeared with the waning glamor of the park.

Greek Candy-Maker in Piedmont ...

George Merras, the Greek candy-maker whose kindness to all and the sweets from whose kitchen have earned his position among the immortals of our story, continued to carry on his business in the tiny room of the neglected Club House even after the park itself had lost its popularity. Here he made his famous divinity and nougat fudge, selling it fresh from the pans to people who came from far and near to use the candy for parties and special gifts, thus brought George a measure of prosperity. When the Civic Center was built, a few years later, the owners arranged for George to occupy the new candy store. This hope was never realized, for sudden death took the little man away from his Piedmont friends. The bronze plaque on the store window of the Sweet Shop today is there to his memory.

Springs Grounds and Wildwood ...

Activity in building was rapidly increasing, as the ever growing desire for hillside homes was fast inducing old friends and neighbors to move from Oakland out to this country above. The "gasoline buggies" were beginning to appear and were able to make better time covering the grades than the horse and carriage. Another fact was that the water system had been improved and electric lighting brought into the homes.

Relative to the eventual acquisition of the Springs Grounds by the City of Piedmont, here are a few names of interest connected with it, previous to Haven's ownership of the tract. The Honorable E. Playter, a mayor of Oakland and the father of Miss Playter and Mrs. Murray Johnson, and a group of men (including T. L. Barker, father of Mrs. Wallace Alexander) had purchased the land, expecting to subdivide it and put it upon the market. But the Havens-Limert Company offered to buy it and was accepted. Hugh Craig strongly opposed the subdivision of this natural beauty spot and appreciated the Havens effort to keep it intact. But when danger again threatened this lovely canyon. Mr. Wallace Alexander bought the property from the mortgage holders, February, 1922, in order to turn it over to the City. A

The Art Gallery in the Park

bond issue later reimbursed Mr. Alexander for the full value of the loan, one hundred and twenty-five thousand dollars, with interest.

After the death of Mrs. Havens, the Wildwood property reverted into the hands of the mortgage holders, and the place remained vacant with a single caretaker about. A project was considered by interested Piedmonters to make it a private club, but financial advisors discouraged such a venture. Finally, in October, 1943, it was sold to Mr. and Mrs. Kohlhaas, who had lived in India, and were able to appreciate this priceless duplication of a Rajah's dwelling, reposing on a hillside in California.

In June, 1953, this unusual home opened wide its doors to welcome the wedding guests who had driven up from St. Paul's Church after the beautiful marriage ceremony uniting the young daughter Marie to Edward Manon. Today, while Mr. and Mrs. Kohlhaas (he has interests in United States Steel) are spending a few years in the Eastern States, their son and his family are putting new life into this Oriental palace in our Queen City.

FIFTH PERIOD—1907-1914

Political Issues Assume Grave Importance . . .

Politics, that controversial subject avoided in drawing rooms where Victorian conventions were observed, were discussed at almost every social gathering. The passing of the stalwart English queen after a reign of sixty years seemed to portend a change in thinking throughout the entire world. There began the breaking away from those comfortable days of well padded luxuries enjoyed in an old-fashioned way. New ideas and outspoken opinions on every subject began to be printed and read in books and magazines. The end of an era had come.

There appeared in these United States the dynamic personality of Theodore Roosevelt, who introduced some new ideas for the old capitalistic system. He favored its extension in an effort to include social sympathies for the less privileged classes and soon became recognized as a Progressive. A fearless man and a forceful speaker, he possessed that personal enthusiasm which was to influence to such a large extent party politics during and after the turn of the century.

Our own State of California produced another courageous leader with progressive ideas. The newssheets of the day were head-lining in large type the name of Hiram Johnson. He, too, dared to speak up for the common people and for new laws to improve their social welfare.

While the governor of California, he had to contend with powerful interests which opposed his actions. As United States Senator he devotedly served California for many years, always adhering steadfastly to his convictions. Like other great leaders in economic and social reforms, he counted both his friends and enemies among the most prominent men of his time.

Local Politics ...

While this political unrest seethed in the country as a whole, it found a fertile field of action in Oakland. Here Major John L. Davie became a powerful figure and wielded an iron control over municipal affairs. Ambitious to increase city boundaries, supporters of this idea set about gaining control of outlying towns and settlements. An especially choice portion of the County land, Piedmont, was to be included in this "Greater Oakland", the slogan adopted by the promoters. Had this movement been permitted to include the group of Piedmont homesites where heretofore only County taxes were paid, the contribution to the larger municipality would have been considerable and the benefits to the smaller, negligible.

In the earliest years of the Twentieth Century the voice from the hill section, that of Hugh Craig, began to be hard in no uncertain terms. He attended the Oakland Council meetings and offered vociferous objections to the idea of bringing Piedmont's residential acreages into and under the domination of a group of politicians.

The larger City had been struggling under questionable influences and graft for a long period, and the foresight of a few Piedmont men became apparent early in 1900, as they perceived the oncoming tide. So, calmly and persistently they worked to discover a means of keeping local government under a control more in harmony with the ideals of a purely residential community.

Struggle Against Incorporation ...

During the intervening years Hugh Craig attended meetings and endeavored to familiarize himself on the surrounding political movements. Mr. James A. Ballantine, another civic-minded Scotsman, served as the legal advisor in the effort to hold out against Piedmont becoming incorporated into "Greater Oakland".

Both Mr. Ballantine and Father made trips to Sacramento to make themselves familiar with the legal status of such a community of homes as they envisioned for the Piedmont hills. Most of those pioneers who had driven their horses out from the stables onto the red rock roads of Piedmont heartily supported this project. Meanwhile, these two men gave gratuitiously of their time and service. It required clever action and counter-attack to "hold out" from becoming a part of the newly annexed territory. Ultimately, the boundary lines of Oakland completely surrounded the Piedmont acres, leaving it to develop into an independent City.

Drawing Up of the Charter . . .

Then commenced the really serious business of organization work and detail. This meant the compilation of the rules and ordinances which had to be observed as soon as the new government began to function. Together Ballantine and Father formulated a City Charter which would be legal and also suitable for the local requirements. Thus they were ready when the year of success finally arrived.

Mr. Louis J. Kennedy, County Assessor, gives the following facts: "Before finality of incorporation could be achieved, a defined border-line had to be decided on and legally approved. Without question the north line of Oakland became the south line of Piedmont, while the east line of Oakland served as the west line of Piedmont. Then the north and east boundaries for the contemplated city were chosen, mapped and plotted to follow a line already established around what was known as the Piedmont Sanitary District of Alameda County. Interested citizens accepted this selection, and it was presented in Sacramento and made legal by an Act of the State Legislature. . .

"The annexing of more territory to the east was then possible but at the time greater expansion seemed prohibitive. In 1909 Oakland annexed all of the surrounding acreages north and east of Piedmont, borderlines, thus closing forever any opportunity for the small city to increase its domain. . ."

According to the Charter under which it now operates, a two-thirds majority vote of the people favoring absorption by adjoining towns is necessary for the dissolution of municipal status.

"Exclusive" and "unique" are adjectives that are now applicable!

Actual Incorporation . . .

The date that may be accepted as the most eventful one in the history of this section of Alameda County is January 30, 1907. For it was this date that witnessed the legal signature to a document which made all of the land within certain designated boundary lines "A Municipal Corporation of the Sixth Class . . . Said City of Piedmont is now a Municipal Corporation, organized and existing under, and by virtue of, an act of the Legislature of the State of California. Approved March 13, 1883.

"The first meeting of the Board of Trustees of the City of Piedmont was held on the eighth day of February, 1907, at the office of the Piedmont Development Club in the City of Piedmont at three o'clock P.M. There were present George Armstrong, Henry A. Butters, Hugh Craig, Varney Gaskill and James A. Ballantine.

"Grant L. Taggart, a Notary Public, in and for the County of Alameda, State of California, administered the oaths of office to Trustees George Armstrong, Henry A. Butters, Hugh Craig, Varney Gaskill and Miles Standish, each of whom took his seat as a member of the Board of Trustees of the City of Piedmont. On motion of Trustee Gaskill, seconded by Trustee Butters, Trustee Craig was unanimously chosen as temporary Chairman of the Board of Trustees, James A. Ballantine acting as Clerk".

The first volume of official records, regarding the early formation of Piedmont's government, now reposes in the vaults of the City Hall on Vista Avenue. From its pages which narrate the happenings of the Council meetings, there can be discerned different opinions as to the advisability of "isolation" for such a small community. Pressure from the politicians of Oakland was wielding a strong influence over one or two members of the Board, and within a few months Varney Gaskill submitted his resignation. This vacancy was filled by Mr. Girvan.

Isolation Becomes Heated Question . . .

The issue became such a point of contention among neighbors that the Council decided to call for a vote of the people on the question of their wish to remain a municipality. The Piedmont Charter stipulates that a two-thirds majority of the voters must be in favor of disincorporation before the erstwhile City can be dissolved or absorbed by any adjoining section.

The date of September 5, 1907, will go down in the annals of Piedmont as the day of its first election. Excitement and emotions ran high. The number of valid ballots cast was 153: 92 of these were in favor of disincorporation, 61 against disincorporation. Two-thirds of 153 would have been 102, the number that would be required to put the scattered group of homes and population back again to County status. The ninety-two votes were not quite sufficient to turn the tide.

The present ten thousand or more citizens of our beloved town can by means of simple arithmetic observe that a mere ten votes preserved for them the permanent right of electing their own governing body. One sees the slim margin by which the City preserved its unique character.

Organization of the Civic Association . . .

Among the loyalists who assisted in the struggle to hold on to the ideals and controls in the new town were Mr. Coop and his son-in-law, Mr. C. U. Martin. They came over to Piedmont in 1904 and built their homes at the corner of Oakland and Bonita Avenues. Today Mr. Martin is doing a necessary and singular service as a long and honored resident. He was the organizer and is the president of a flourishing Civic Association, to which every person living within the Piedmont boundary line is invited to join in order to have a voice in the progressive advance of good government. A city without a Chamber of Commerce needs such an open-minded, democratic group as Mr. Martin has organized.

Problems of City Government . . .

The problems of today may seem appalling, but those five Trustees in 1907 faced responsibilities of tremendous import. With a pitifully small amount of tax money on hand they initiated work on a necessary and constructive program directed towards the improvement of local conditions. But the people across the countryside suddenly demanded paved roads, here and there a few sidewalks, also an adequate sewerage system, better water service and even a policeman on horseback! Firemen and important equipment had to await an increase in treasury funds.

One dependable man, Chris Jensen, of Danish descent, served these early Councilmen in many different capacities. As a young man he had come to be foreman on the Walter Blair ranch and had of late years resided on the lower portion of the property inherited by Miss Lizzie Blair. Chris, as everybody called him, owned and drove the heavy span of horses which drew the watering cart as it sprinkled down the red dust on Moraga Road and along Vernal Avenue.

The new officers would frequently call on Chris when questions arose regarding contours of hills and ravines that might govern the dispo-

Japanese Tea Garden in the Park

sition of water sheds and drainage. He knew every acre of land and the people whose homes he took pride in protecting. If a horse or cow or skittish calf happened to get adrift, and wander into strange pastures, it was always Chris who knew the owner and the particular knack of leading it homeward.

"Single Tax" and Henry George . . .

Real estate improvements were now encouraged and were assuming the utmost importance. Every lot on which the owner erected a home brought the prescribed tax money into the constantly depleted treasury coffers. However, these meager sums were far from adequate to meet the expanding needs. The few employees were poorly paid, for a careful watch had to be maintained over every outlay of money.

Responsibility fell heavily upon Mayor Hugh Craig, and it became imperative that he acquaint himself with various systems and theories of municipal taxation and with the theories of recognized economists. On the library table in the Craig home lay books and pamphlets, marked and underscored, relating to this subject. Among those studied was an erudite treatise, written in 1878 by the American economist and lecturer, Henry George, on the pro and con arguments of the single tax movement.

Quoting briefly, Henry George urged the extension of "social sympathies to the lower classes . . . People should work: a capital should invest, and no owner should have the power to withhold resources . . . More concretely, every family has a right to a homestead plot; no individual has the privilege of withholding from use more of God's bounty than he can actually use . . . Historically, as well as ethically, private property in land is robbery." These are only a few of his premises and theories to which the several members of the Council gave consideration. The approach to the problem of adjusted taxation became of paramount importance, and they adopted a new policy which shortly brought forth distress calls of protest from the holders of acreage properties.

As soon as incorporation had become a reality, many far-sighted realtors and men of means had recognized the future increase in values which was certain to occur upon these hillsides. Therefore, large parcels were acquired from the early farmers or from the banks holding lands through the foreclosures of mortgages. The purchasers expected to make a profit of considerable proportions within a few years. In the interim they were paying a very low tax: the old rate of County assessment. But the people who were building the ten, twelve and fifteen thousand dollar homes on modest fifty foot lots had to pay for the initial improvements that enhanced the sale price on the larger holdings.

Inauguration of the New Tax System . . .

The years between 1907 and 1914 witnessed the inauguration of a tax program which seemed just and equitable in the minds of the majority of Piedmont home owners. Its application brought in the extra revenue needed so desperately to cover the minimum budget for the struggling City. A fair proportion of this initial expense was levied upon the larger tracts. It might be well to state at this point the fact that the increased rates on large holdings were in like manner applied to the Craig six acres, also to the twenty-acre Requa estate and other pieces owned by early settlers. They realized the extent of the City requirements and cooperated by paying the heavier taxes.

With his background of experience as a Director, followed by three years as president of the San Francisco Chamber of Commerce, Hugh Craig had developed his ability as a public speaker, enabling him to present his theories in an understandable manner to his constituents while carrying out this scheme of taxation. But in so doing he antagonized and alienated the very men with whom he had always held pleasant associations. His once lucrative fire and marine insurance business began to dwindle, a goodly number of the large premiums having come from these same associates. Father's integrity was never questioned, but his positive manner often provoked undue controversy. Neither money nor social prestige could induce him to "play along" with anyone if his conscience dictated otherwise.

During these first seven years, the coming to maturity period of our City, there appeared numerous civic improvements and the erection of many fine homes. (1) However, the controversies in Piedmont through this period caused the formation of a powerful group of men who assumed control of the City government in 1914, with an authority that lasted through the next twenty-five years.

---

(1) Cf. Appendix III for these additions.

Harsh Traffic Regulations ...

If this is to be a complete record covering factual occurrences, there must appear a fleeting note of discord: another reflection of similar happenings elsewhere. The trustees were searching for new ways of bringing dollars into the treasury by every known legal means and finally hit upon a clever scheme. Automobiles were found in ever-increasing numbers, and it is easy to recall the advertisements that shrieked their claims about high speed cars. The owners of these fast cars liked the drive from Oakland and on to Vernal Avenue, where they could "let 'er out" to a rate of sixty miles an hour. Many of these pacemakers were from Piedmont families.

For the safety of its citizens and in order to prevent runaways (terrified horses stampeding with their helpless drivers in the carriage behind) the controlling Board decreed that the drivers of these cars should not exceed a given speed, or the violators should be subjected to the penalty of a severe fine. This precept was announced in the local paper. Police were then alerted, and in an improvised courtroom a youthful judge suddenly became very busy imposing the heavy penal fines.

Resentment was soon aroused, and this may have had some effect upon the later hostility that developed over the tax rates. Officiousness and ridicule exercised by those in power frequently act as boomerangs, and others with more tactful methods will supplant them. Such was the result in the present instance.

The Municipal Elections of 1914 ...

The newly arrived citizenry of Piedmont were mostly families of wealth and established social position. Many of them had lived as neighbors in Oakland and were close friends. Rapidly they were filling up the hills, buying desirable lots, building handsome homes and furnishing them with the appropriate accessories for fashionable entertainment.

While the taxes on such estates rated less than in the adjoining city, some of these property holders were ill-pleased with the Council's revised levy and with the power exercised over municipal affairs. This contingent of old friends desired to gain among themselves that power wielded by a majority membership on the Board.

From the minutes of the meeting of the Board of Trustees, April 20, 1914, we read:

"A special meeting of the Board of Trustees of the City of Piedmont was held at the City Hall in the City of Piedmont on Monday, April 20, 1914, at eight o'clock, PM, pursuant to law, for the purpose of canvassing the votes cast at the general municipal election for city officers held on Monday, the thirteenth day of June, 1914.

"There were present Trustees Church, Farr, Munson, Starr, and Craig. Trustee Craig, President of the Board of Trustees, presided at the meeting, and James A. Ballantine, City Clerk, acted as such.

"President Craig announced the purpose of the meeting and the Board proceeded to canvas the votes cast at the general election held on April 13, 1914, and upon completion of the canvas, President Craig announced the results as follows, to wit:

"Elected for Trustee, Oliver Ellsworth 464
     ”   ”   ”   Walter A. Starr 427
     ”   ”   ”   Laurence F. Moore 373
     ”   ”   ”   Roderic W. Church .... 271"

The Changing of the Guard . . .

This election left Craig and Farr to continue in their terms of office, and Starr was re-elected to the full term along with Ellsworth and Moore as the new members, thus wresting the majority rule from the old guard. Trustee Ellsworth was immediately elected President of the Board. Trustee Starr thereupon moved that a vote of thanks be extended to Trustee Craig for his long and efficient services as President of the Board. Trustee Moore seconded the motion and it was adpoted by a unanimous vote.

Trustee Ellsworth, the new President of the Board, then addressed Mr. Craig and the new and retiring members of the Board, plus the large lobby in attendance. He spoke at length in praise of Mr. Craig's faithful and untiring services to the City of Piedmont during the seven years of his presidency. Mr. Craig's retirement from the office meant the loss to the City of Piedmont of a valuable officer.

"Mr. Craig then thanked the Board for the compliments paid him and tendered his resignation as Trustee to take effect immediately . . . On motion of Trustee Moore, seconded by Trustee Starr, the meeting was adjourned."

Entrance of the Wallace Alexanders . . .

In writing of Piedmont one finds that interest centers more around the people who have made the place famous, rather than upon the rolling hills now dotted with homes. This is as it should be, for scenes lose their magic with familiarity and changing conditions. But people with their varied characteristics never cease to inspire us with admiration, interest and often perplexity.

About the close of the fourth period of our story, during the eventful year of 1906, the young Wallace Alexanders came into the community. Their prominence and generosity extended over a generation, becoming a constructive and dominating influence in the City's progress. Both the husband and wife were from pioneer Oakland families. Samuel Thomas Alexander had acquired large sugar holdings on the Island of Maui, in the Hawaiian group, and the son, Wallace, was born there on November 10, 1869. He had three sisters who were also born on the sugar plantation.

The parents decided to bring their children to the mainland for education in the private schools of Oakland. Their home at Sixteenth and Filbert Streets soon became a social center for young people. Only a few blocks to the east of the Alexander menage lived the Timothy Barkers at the corner of Castro and Thirteenth Streets. From there in 1904, their only daughter Mary became Mrs. Wallace Alexander.

After a short period of residence in San Francisco the couple decided to seek a quiet home on the hills of the East Bay, particularly after the earthquake and fire wrought such devastating destruction on San Francisco.

Frustration at First Brings Ultimate Satisfaction...

The tale of their selection of the homesite upon which they finally settled comes directly from Mrs. Alexander herself. Riding in an open horse-drawn buggy, Mr. and Mrs. Alexander drove up the winding red-rock roads to the acreage owned by the late Judge E. B. Crocker. The land had just recently been surveyed and offered for sale. It still remained in a primitive state, however, with squirrel holes undermining the top soil, dotting it over with hummocks of soil thrown out by the little animals.

After the Alexanders had decided upon a certain location, they drove to Walter Leimert's real estate office, newly erected upon a corner of the tract. To their astonishment another couple had just preceded them and had signed up for precisely the same piece of land. These were the Henry Nichols, soon destined to be among Piedmont's leading citizens. Mrs. Nichols was a granddaughter of the late Hiram

Tubbs, who in earlier days brought fame to East Oakland by the popularity of the large hostelry known as Tubbs Hotel.

Undaunted, the Wallace Alexanders retraced the bumpy roads they had just covered, and they selected an even more advantageous site adjoining the Nichols' southern boundary. Upon the broad knoll of this acreage soon they constructed a home from which radiated friendly hospitality in the following decades.

Other Families Follow These Trail Blazers ...

The sloping fields about the house quickly reflected the skill of competent landscape gardeners. Redwoods, which so truly belong to the California setting, were set out along the upper boundary, and at their base a gentle rivulet trickled down to the flower beds below, fashioned after nature's own design. Around its twisting curves and among the rocks appeared delicate ferns, intermingled with forget-me-nots and pansies and other bright spots of color. With the establishment of the Alexander home upon these heights facing the Golden Gate, many other families from Oakland found their way to Leimert's real estate office, and new homes were planned to fit into the contours of the various locations.

The senior Mrs. Alexander built a spacious home on the high corner across Sea View Avenue from that of her son. Also, Mrs. Wallace Alexander's mother established her residence a block further up on Sea View Avenue. In close proximity to these friends the Walter Starrs bought a large corner lot on which they developed a garden of rare shrubbery surrounding their home.

One of the earliest mansions to arise on the Crocker tract was built in the center of the block bounded by Crocker, Hampton and King Avenues. The late Mrs. Florence Blythe Hinckley, who had just then become Mrs. A. A. Moore, purchased the site, and she too had groups of redwood trees planted on the lower slopes. In later years these were to afford privacy and seclusion to the R. Stanley Dollars, who purchased the estate in 1920.

Formation of Piedmont Community Church ...

Coincident with the advent of the Alexanders into Piedmont, the new City government received papers of incorporation, dated January 7, 1907. Then began the effort to obtain better roads, construction of sidewalks, lighting and adequate disposal systems, and many of the other demands of the fast developing town. To these civic enterprises Mr. Alexander gave his unfailing support. Particularly did he contribute to the community effort in the maintenance of Mowbray Hall as a center for Sunday school and other gatherings of a religious nature.

In the course of the years, Mr. and Mrs. Alexander purchased a vacant lot with a frontage curving around the corner of Highland and Mountain Avenues. A group of citizens then formed themselves into a corporation and with Mr. Albert Farr as architect an artistic row of three stores was built facing the park. Upon the higher ground a commodious church of Spanish design completed this focal point of community interest. The courtyard of this church is surrounded by lower buildings used for Sunday School and various club activities.

All Protestant denominations were represented on the Board of Trustees which formed this church organization in 1916 and called it the Piedmont Interdenominational Church. A more recent decision has shortened the title to Piedmont Community Church.

Then ensued a length of time during which the early residents of the town were slow to respond to the innovation of a religious center for all faiths. They preferred to travel the distance into Oakland to their more familiar places of worship. However, Mr. and Mrs. Alexander maintained an interest in and gave generous support to the project during those lean years. Various groups were gradually formed among the women who worked for charitable and cutural purposes. Then too, as the more youthful population increased, the idea of a single church for all denominations gained in popularity.

Birth of Piedmont's Boy Scouts . . .

With so many children growing into young adulthood the need for Boy Scouting became apparent to Mr. Alexander, and he sponsored and founded that organization in Piedmont. Later their beloved founder gave to these boys the mountain playground, known today as Camp Wallace Alexander.

In 1914 at the outbreak of World War I Mrs. Alexander organized and equipped the Red Cross Chapter of the East Bay. Her home served as a center for meetings and work, and she has maintained her membership over the years and continued as honorary president of this organization during the Second World War.

As Piedmont grew in population, the importance of the City increased in proportion. Mr. Alexander's foresight and wise judgement

Hugh Craig—1907

became a dominating influence and control over the Board of Trustees, as he continued to render aid in the betterment of conditions. But this outstanding citizen of Piedmont was called by Death, November 28, 1939. In the Piedmont Community Church on the following Sunday a memorial tribute service was held for this philanthropist. Attending the crowded services were many business associates from San Francisco, members of clubs and associations with which he had been connected and those who had known and revered him as a friend and neighbor.

Mrs. Alexander's Disposition of the Home . . .

After the loss of her husband Mrs. Alexander did not find it easy to continue the same life alone in the large home. The young daughter Martha had attended the Ransom-Bridges School and later Stanford University. Since graduation she had married Dr. Frank L. A. Gerbode and was now residing in San Francisco with her little family.

After due consideration Mrs. Alexander decided to have her Piedmont home, wrapped as it was in happy memories, razed to the ground and allow the property with its lovely gardens to be subdivided into appropriate sized lots. More families could then enjoy the privilege of owning a home upon the hills.

With this purpose firmly in mind Mrs. Alexander offered the grounds to the Community Church as the setting for a Sunday afternoon concert, previous to the date for the sad conflagration. A heavenly day in mid-Summer, 1940, dawned as a fitting background for the final swan song of the Alexander home. The audience was composed of the friends and neighbors and were filled with sentimental thoughts at this farewell gathering, although Mrs. Alexander herself did not feel strong enough to make an appearance.

Memories Inspired by the Setting . . .

Thoughts ran pell-mell through my mind, but the principal feeling that haunted me was that I, who was a little girl and had played and picnicked upon these very fields and had gathered into the emptied lunch basket the yellow cowslips and white puff-balls, should be sitting there that day. My thoughts continued on the same retrospective lines: These wild flowers were to be found among the treasured buttercups, lupine and poppies, as they formed the majestic Spring carpet over the Crocker tract acres. The spot where that Sunday afternoon concert was being given I had frequently selected as the favorite Saturday playground, and we would continue on down into Indian Gulch, where maiden hair fern grew in abundance along the stream. And now, fifty years later, I sat on that Sunday afternoon amid the man-made landscaping created during the past decades, but still I was under the same blue sky and enjoying the fragrant afternoon sunshine. My life seemed to have come its full circle that day.

Accompanied by piano and violin, the clear voices of the choir floated out over the concourse of people, many of whom were filled with emotion, while savoring the happy memories of earlier parties in this same lovely garden. The events of that afternoon seemed to portend the close of one era and the beginning of another with its result not yet disclosed.

Greater opportunities for a larger number of people were in the offing. This is the eminent sign of a slow process of evolution, evidenced in the mental attitudes of the controlling powers toward the oppressed peoples all over the world.

The life of Mr. Wallace Alexander and his wife has indicated their desire to keep in tune with cultural and economic progression towards the gradual improvement and welfare of mankind. Their years of residence upon these hills will always remain a loving memory among the citizens of Piedmont.

SIXTH PERIOD—1914-1945

The Starting of a New Regime . . .

The Board of Trustees with Mr. Ellsworth as Mayor took over the directive policies of Piedmont in April, 1914, as mentioned earlier. These trustees were imbued with enthusiasm and constructive ideas for the town in which most of them had come so recently to reside. The foundation laid by the pioneers had builded for a sound basis for future development, but with the evolution of progress the older methods must give way to the ideas of the new majority group who have acquired the power of government.

Under the efficient leadership of Mayor Ellsworth, who succeeded Hugh Craig, the Board of Trustees could proceed with all civic affairs including the adjustment of taxes, according to the policies and wishes of those whom they represented. Quietly and in an orderly fashion tax rates were changed and plans made for a privately owned business section in the City. Food, drug and candy stores comprised this first unit of the Civic Center. They were greatly needed and were welcomingly acclaimed by all the residents.

The Council possessed the right to restrict the encroachment of any further business concerns in the municipality. However, as new demands became apparent, the private corporation which owned the Civic Center property allowed the Standard Oil Company of California to install one of its well equipped stations. A few years later a bank building was erected adjoining the stores, and this was leased out to the American Trust Company. Not long after that a real estate office and a barber shop made their appearance, neatly tucked along side of the gas station and at the rear of the bank, making it all a very substantial unit of income property.

Sale of "Piedmont Acres" ...

The name of Louis Titus became associated with real estate transactions on the Indian Gulch slopes, bordering Piedmont's eastern boundary lines. Mr. Titus planned a large mansion for himself and his wife upon the knoll where now reside the Jean Witter family. The most pretentious ideas had been conceived for developing an estate, and the balance of the unimproved land was later to be sold at a much higher figure.

However, the increased valuation placed on such properties by the prevailing city tax rate forced Mr. Titus to abandon his grandiose schemes, and he sold a choice parcel of forty acres to James Tyson in 1914. Robert Tyson, a brother of James, had already built a home on the corner of Mountain and Sea View Avenues, and along with Titus and other large land holders he had joined forces to crush the Craig ideal of taxation. These cohorts succeeded in securing a majority of members in the Council who were committed to a more flexible policy of assessment.

Tyson Real Estate Improvements ...

An ambitious and dynamic personality seemed to motivate the actions of James Tyson, who ordered men, teams, plows and trucks to proceed with quick dispatch on the surveying, grading and building projects instituted by his recent acquisition of the real estate property. This rugged corner, barely within the city's highest boundary line, needed a roadway to be carved through its fields in order to make its varied residential sites more accessible.

Hampton Road, named in honor of Mrs. Tyson's parents, formed the southern boundary of their property, while on its western side the curving Sotello Avenue led to a front gate from which location a driveway wound around the hill, finally reaching the spacious and warmly hospitable home. Across the canyon below a dam had been constructed by these interests to catch the winter's rains, thus forming a sizable reservoir of water.

After the Tysons, with their sons, Lawrence, James and John, moved over from Alameda, this lake became a favorite swimming hole for all of the neighborhood boys, and the surrounding land was made into a camping ground for the Boy Scouts.

Mr. Tyson also permitted another portion of his estate to be used by the National Guard. Lawrence Tyson, the eldest son, was an active member of the Guard, until his untimely death in 1926 took a splendid young man from his family and associates.

Allen L. Chickering Enters the Piedmont Arena ...

Another choice acreage on the east side of Highland Avenue, directly opposite the Park, lay ready for development. From the picture taken on a bright Sunday morning in early September, 1903, there can be observed in the foreground a turn-stile, which pointed the way for the present Sierra Avenue in the "heart of Piedmont". On this scenic, winding street resides today an esteemed citizen who is recognized in cultural and business circles as a leading figure on both sides of the Bay.

As a youngster Allen L. Chickering probably twirled through this rural contraption, trod the plank walk, and ran across the Richardson-Wing cow pasture, and then tramped over other fields on his way to the wilder and more forested hills. Here, with his gun cocked and ready he would make short shrift of any squirrels and quail which he spied down the gun sights. Little did this eager huntsman think that one day he would be a big game hunter.

The years fled by, and in 1912 Mr. and Mrs. Chickering were living in a modern home surrounded by formal gardens and fashioned upon the open fields where only a short while previously wild flowers had blossomed in generous profusion. A bed of these native flowers is now one of the principal features of the back garden of his home.

The pioneer record of this family extends back through several generations, and Mr. Chickering has stimulated a widespread interest in the California Historical Society, of which he has been the President for several years.

At some unforeseen and unsuspected moment there comes into almost every home the darkening shadow of a sorrow and parting. His son, William Henry Chickering left Piedmont at the last call to war as a war correspondent and reporter of no little note. During the conflict he was assigned to follow the course of warfare over the wide, boundless spaces of the Pacific. Finally at the battle for Lingayan Gulf a bomb exploded near him and killed him. This was a poignant blow to his family and friends who saw in him such promise and hope. But among other things he had written a most delightful book for all to enjoy, *Within the Sound of These Waves,* in which he wrote most movingly about Hawaii. Here is a quotation from its epilogue: "Still the old spirit lives on deep in the hearts of the Hawaiian people, that rare humor and kindliness and love of living." In a personal message of condolence, General Douglas MacArthur radioed that William Henry Chickering was "a correspondent, a gentleman and a soldier."

The Moffit Name Added to Piedmont Citizens ...

In about 1910 a lady well known in both San Francisco and in the East Bay, Mrs. James Moffitt, decided to place her name on the list of Piedmont taxpayers. She purchased the property on the west side of Sea View Avenue, adjacent to the Wallace Alexander estate. Here on this lovely slope with a view directly across the Golden Gate, Mrs. Moffitt built her new home with its spacious rooms and wide verandahs overlooking the dry poppy fields. A lovely garden soon blossomed forth, and only a fence of flowers separated it from the Alexander neighbors to the south.

The old Moffitt estate on Broadway, Webster and Twenty-Second Streets was rapidly being surrounded by business firms. The two daughters, Mrs. John H. Lynch and Mrs. George Doubleday, had been married from this long established home and were now living in New York State. But with her genial personality and host of friends Mrs. Moffitt soon filled the new home with activity and happiness.

Within a very few years her son, James K. Moffitt, bought a very choice piece of property directly opposite his mother's land, preparatory to building a home for the lovely Pauline Fore Moffitt, whom he had married in 1907. She will be well remembered as the "most beautiful girl in Oakland". The Fore family lived on Franklin Street

Mrs. Hugh Craig—1907

next to the old Sharon house, and all of the sisters were noted for their beauty and sweetness of character.

The large one-story house which Mr. and Mrs. Moffitt built a few years later was the first to rise on the east side of Sea View Avenue. Their grounds extended down to the ravine known in earlier days as Indian Gulch, through which a bubbling brook still runs. The banks have been terraced and laid out with intriguing paths through shrubbery and choice flowers which make a blaze of color in season. The young daughter Genevieve has frequently been hostess for the Children's Hospital benefits held in the gardens of her parents' home.

Mr. Moffitt is recognized among literary men for his large library of fine and rare books. Also, it can truly be said that he is known to many for his quiet acts of generosity in Piedmont and elsewhere .(1)

Subdividing the Old Properties ...

During the years preceding World War I economic upheavals over the entire globe began to cast their approaching shadows over this rapidly growing city. Prosperity was increasing for many families, but for others there was signaled the sudden drop from heights often painfully attained. The gradual changes were a progressive continuation of the process that had started when the enormous private ranches along the coastal area of California were divided by the Spanish dons into smaller parcels. These went into the ownership of numerous farmers, and they in turn had to give way to the estates of the well-to-do business man of the day.

Now, in 1910, after a decade of rather luxurious living the home owners of the local acreages felt the severe pinch of the increased tax rates and began to heed the demand for more building sites of moderate size. According to an old map of the Wickham Havens Real Estate Company, portions of the Craig and Sharon properties were listed for sale, with Dennis Dimond acting as salesman. Mr. Dimond was married to Madeline Sterling, sister of George Sterling and cousin to the Havens.

The Sharon frontage on Mountain Avenue was soon sold. On one of these new lots the daughter Florence, then Mrs. Herbert Hamilton Brown, built a large house, while another lot was selected by Captain I. A. Thayer. In close proximity came Mrs. Cleveland

(1) Cf. Appendix for social note about Mrs. Moffitt.

Baker, whose maiden name was Pansy Perkins, daughter of California's honored United States Senator, George C. Perkins. Mrs. Baker's homesite is now the residence of the well known eye-specialist, Dr. Raymond Nutting.

In plotting the Craig property, the original map was followed. Vita Avenue, running through it north and south, would allow the house to remain where it was then located. Fortunately, no sales were made, and after deeper consideration the family felt that a pressing need existed for an artery to connect Mountain Avenue in a direct line with Highland Avenue. Increased traffic from the higher regions would cause congestion as it moved around the circuitous route via the Park and Civic Center.

Subdivision of the Craig Estate ...

The Craigs then had another survey made and planned the street to run east and west this time. This meant the moving of the house to another location. The lot best suited to the "transplanting" of that bulky structure seemed to be down in the orchard. It was a tremendous task, undertaken and successfully completed by the reputable firm of the Henderson Brothers. They even managed to keep intact three large brick chimneys, which had withstood the earthquake of 1906. The cost of this move, plus a new foundation, exceeded five thousand dollars. That was only the beginning, though. Then came the grading, cutting and paving of the street, costing another five thousand dollars. Both these outlays were completely paid for by the family. Also, the considerable square footage made into the street became of benefit to the City. Hugh Craig, as Mayor, would receive no reimbursement from the depleted municipal treasury.

Every city includes part of its local history in the naming of its streets, and Craig Avenue retains the memory of its donor.

Buyers in the "Heart of Piedmont" ...

Most of the handsome estates of this period have disappeared, while others are marked by the process of change. Here is a glimpse of the first of such subdivisions. "In the Heart of Piedmont" was the phrase coined by the William J. Laymance Company as the sales slogan for the Craig tract. One of the first lots sold went to Dr. Guy Liliencrantz and his wife, who had been Flora Sterling. Both were from early Piedmont families. They built a lovely home and had the well known

Julia Morgan as architect. But in a few years the doctor found that it was more convenient to live in Oakland, so their house was sold.

Soon thereafter, Miss Juliet Alexander selected two lots on Craig Avenue, and here architects and builders created a spreading bungalow, designed about an inner central court, filled with flowers and ferns converging upon an ornate fountain after the Hawaiian fashion. This garden covered the extra land facing Oakland Avenue.

Another house rating among the first to be built on this newly opened subdivision was one built by the Chris Jorgensens for their daughter Aimee, one of the Ghirardelli descendants. Aimee was the joyous bride of a fine young man from New England, Ralph Andersen. But a year or two later the tragic death of the young wife left a bereaved family and an infant son, Chris Andersen, who is now married and carrying on the line of progeny.

In the course of the years the balance of these lots were sold, and the artery soon became a much travelled thoroughfare for those driving down from the hills to the east.

Death of Mrs. Requa (1922) ...

A finale to the elaborate social affairs that belonged to the decade when the buttercup-yellow mansion ruled supreme over these hills was reached at Mrs. Requa's ninety-third birthday party. A smiling lady greeted old friends and neighbors with all the grace and formality of earlier years. She was elegantly gowned in brocade and satin, a garment resonant of former days when its rustle had been heard at a Sacramento inaugural ball. probably at the commencement of the late Stanford's term of office.

This gathering within the Highland gateway seemed to foretell an auspicious occasion, like a reception of the Past in its gayest and most elaborate setting. The old house looked like an old patriarch regarding with timeless and kindly eyes all who passed through its doors. One realized that its walls had resounded with many scenes enacted by three successive generations of family life. In the dining room a huge birthday cake, decorated with ninety-three lighted candles, adorned the center of the long table, creating in all present a deep and lasting impression.

But a brief year or so later, in 1922, on a dreary December day, the flower-laden hearse moved out of the black and gold gateway. A grand

and kindly old lady was taken from the Piedmont scene, in which for nearly fifty years she had been a dominating and uplifting force.

The Cupola Topples . . .

To place a definite period to Mrs. Requa's passing, drama, real drama, took place shortly before noon on a bright summer day in 1923. Doubtless, few but the hardened wreckers themselves witnessed the actual fall of the cupola from atop the Requa house.

However, while casually gazing out of a second-story window across the greenery of the Springs Park, a Craig Avenue neighbor noticed the movements of workers, scaffolds and ropes being manipulated on the roof of the old house not far away. Watching in fascination, the neighbor looked closer, for word had quickly gone around that the family was soon going to have the mansion completely razed. In all its years one mistress had ruled the house, and the son and daughter held it sacred to her memory. So, viewing the activities from my excellent vantage point, I was witness to the dramatic scene which definitely gave impetus to the writing of this local history.

The wreckers had planned well and with accuracy. Ropes and men soon had the cupola swaying unsteadily; then it fell with a resounding and splintering crash. Something of youth fell with it and tears came unbidden. Since earliest memory it had been a daily sight and a landmark of home and security. Now, like the rest of this mutable life, the big house was being demolished, and another subdivision soon would be carved out of the beautiful twenty-acre estate.

Requa Road, generously wide and equipped with handsome electroliers, today curves through what was the estate, making it one of the finest sections within the City limits. All of the lots are large and building restrictions are high.

Glimpses into the Roaring Twenties . . .

The sharp but short-lived deflationary period immediately following the close of World War I produced no dent in the economy of our "exclusive" City: Civic affairs were running according to a firm and well ordered pattern. A revised City Charter gave to the Council the legal authority to forbid dwellings of more than one unit to function within the limits of Piedmont. This was designed to rule out apartment houses or flats. A new zoning ordinance forbade the increase of any business concerns above those already permitted to occupy the privately owned section zoned for this specific purpose. Under the efficient direction of Major Oliver Ellsworth the forthcoming era of good times began to bloom all over the green hills of Piedmont.

The single primary school under its able Principal, Miss Ellen Driscoll, was very overcrowded, and all parents were clamoring for more schools. The town was fairly humming with enthusiastic youth. During the free hours for recreation, the daring of these youngsters took them dashing around the curving streets in "Dad's" car or possibly in an obsolete but "souped up" model of their own.

The Occupational Dangers of the Flaming Youth ...

At the lunch period this sheer exuberance of spirits was particularly noticeable on the sidewalks and steps out in front of Hamby's and Cheatham's stores. It would behoove those mothers who braved that shopping hour to step carefully over discarded ends of ice cream cones and banana and orange peels. Courtesy and manners seemed to have gone the way of the defunct horse-and-buggies. These young people evidently felt that the town was theirs, and the most important desire to be fulfilled was that of having fun.

The high school boasted its own cliques of social clubs for both boys and girls and not to belong meant the greatest tragedy imaginable for many students. These exclusive cliques within the school precincts have recently been ruled illegal by action of the State Legislature.

Across the deep, narrow ravine below the public school could often be heard the gay voices of the Ransom girls, sounding through the dense growth of pine and oaks. Strict rules and regulations combined with supervised, constructive diversions, kept these girls constantly occupied. One of the outstanding annual activities, for example, was a full-dress performance of a Shakespearian drama that was presented out beneath the stars, and this play required much study and rehearsal far in advance of the eventful evening in late Spring. Professional training and sincere effort made a finished performance, delighting the parents and friends who had foregathered in the sheltered court facing the main building.

In this same court of the Ransom-Bridges School the yearly graduation exercises were held on a balmy afternoon in mid-June. The girls, clad in their crisp white pleated skirts and flawless middies which were topped by bright yellow silk ties, made a lovely picture of blooming womanhood. Soft strains of a violin played the "Triumphal

March" from Verdi's *Aida,* as the graduates came with measured tread over the winding paths from their schoolrooms to take their places in the seats of honor before the proud assemblage.

Scouting Troops Grow in Popularity ...

Thus, a very evident need for diversional youth occupations became apparent, especially to the elder citizens, and caused the Boy Scout and Girls Scout troops to grow in popularity and in demand. With property then obtainable at a comparatively nominal figure the City Fathers failed to recognize the future growing needs for a general recreational center and playground. They had so carefully and securely fenced in the Springs Park that very few visitors could enjoy its beauties or even observe the uninviting entrances to it. The most desirable corner at Highland and Vista Avenues, immediately adjoining Mowbray Hall, could have been purchased for a nominal sum, because it was owned by an aged and needy widow who wished to sell the property with only the tiny old cottage on it. The Council, however, was so preoccupied with its own headlong pursuits that it ignored the signs of the times.

The dominant motive of those who controlled the City Politic seemed to be to hold the tax rate down and to keep competitive interests from disturbing in any manner the privately owned Civic Center. Another depressive factor was that all public gatherings were discouraged, thus retaining all social life within the individual estates. Only after the Great Depression of the thirties was heed given to these multitudinous requests and was thinking placed on a broader basis for the better administration of municipal affairs.

The Waterfront "Scare" of 1934 ...

Now there comes to mind an episode which for a few dark and tense weeks produced great excitement within the boundary lines of this so-called city of wealth. During the summer of 1934, a period of grave labor unrest, a general strike was called effective throughout the Bay region. It seemed to be largely caused by the harsh marine and waterfront conditions prevalent at this time, and the homes of several big shipping men living in Piedmont at the time had been threatened with bombing.

Of course, such dangers would extend to other residents in the vicinity and, indeed, menace entire neighborhoods. With the usually peaceful city thus endangered, citizens met in private conclaves, and the Council proceeded to swear in as Special Officers brave husbands and fathers ready to protect to the last man their homes and hearths. Out of dark hideaways were produced prized weapons of war to be polished and made ready for active duty. Headquarters were soon settled at Mowbray Hall. Chairs were shoved back to the walls, making space for army cots where these weary vigilantes could catch a few winks of sleep between hours of duty. Here also the ladies came, carrying the hot coffee and sandwiches with which their noble protectors would be sustained.

Every entrance to the City had been immediately barricaded to keep out all suspicious or idle persons, and a strong contingent of extra police, garbed in an assorted array of hunting coats and jackets, took over at each of these focal points. At Highland and Mountain Avenues an extra barricade was erected to guard the Civic Center from any threatened violence. Across both thoroughfares was a strange collection of orange and apple boxes standing on end, connected crudely together by a conglomeration of boards and planks garnered from neighbors' basements. When an automobile or even a pedestrian approached, one of the guards leaped to his feet and with a hand placed carressingly on the handle of his gun, learned the reason for such arrant intrusion.

The outstanding bravery of Lowell Hardy and his deputies kept this important intersection alert at all hours. Affairs looked rather ominous during a few of those days, despite the overtones reminescent of a light opera; the quiet, indeed, seemed foreboding and portentous. But somehow a feeling of peace and security pervaded my home, and with my daughter I remained alone in that big house close to this center.

A few amusing incidents are recalled as occurring in those days of tension and excitement. For instance, a prominent citizen who had been out of town when the emergency edicts went into effect returned in the darkness of the night. He was speeding straight for Magnolia Avenue, when suddenly loud shouts of "Halt!" rent the midnight hush. Forced to slow down, the driver saw the muzzles of four guns flashing in the headlights of the car. Then much to everyone's relief there was mutual recognition. The returnee received an unforgettable welcome that night!

Another story concerns the plight of three landrymen grimly determined to get into the city by fair means or foul to deliver their packages. In less than ten minutes the one-way radio had passed on the news, and the frantic drivers were safely corralled. They tried each

Canyon View of *Wildwood*

exit, but were abruptly turned away at every barricade. Finally, the regular police led them up to the jail, charged with disturbing the peace with the bail of twenty dollars on each head. After some hours of uneasy confinement, their employers arrived with cash in hand to clear up the mess and led the boys off.

Several other humorous incidents occurred, but space does not permit their telling at present. Suffice it to say that our present Chief Pflaum captained his squads most skillfully, dispersing each shadow before it could assume terrifying proportions of reality. After a ten-day patrol the officialdom of Piedmont were all too glad to return to their accustomed pursuits, and all became quiet once again.

PIEDMONT COMMUNITY ORGANIZATIONS AND CLUBS

First Sunday School in Piedmont ...

Piedmont's first religious gathering of known record began with thirty children who had hitherto been aimlessly seeking diversions and companionship on Sunday afternoon. The long drives to Oakland Sunday schools had become irksome to parents and pupils alike, yet all felt the need for Bible lessons of some description.

The First Presbyterian Church at Fourteenth and Franklin Streets in Oakland had a very large attendance at their Sunday school which assembled at the hour of twelve-thirty, immediately after the close of the church services. Its primary department was presided over by Miss Mabel Gray, later known as Mrs. Thomas Mitchell Potter of Piedmont. Assisting her with the little tots were girls who had come from Mrs. H. B. Smith's class in the senior division, and I was numbered in this group.

Mrs. Smith, fully cognizant of the anxiety expressed by Piedmonters for some form of Christian services out in the hill section where the car line ended, consented to give the Bible instructions, provided that it could be arranged for half past three in the afternoon. Mrs. H. C. Capwell, residing in her new home on Oakland Avenue above Pleasant Valley, had been an enthusiastic advocate of a Sunday school and assured the attendance of her three small children. Mrs. Berkenfeld offered the use of two large rooms in the high basement front of her home on Vernal Avenue.

The procurement of funds and equipment was assigned to me a

Mrs. Smith's assistant. Quickly the news spread among the neighbors and the five, ten and twenty dollar gold pieces literally fell into the collection bag of Sunday School funds. Mrs. Isaac L. Requa, Mrs. Frank Havens, Mrs. Capwell, Mrs. Bratnober, Mrs. Sharon, Mrs. Richardson, Mrs. Wing, Mrs. Hugh Craig and Mr. Robert Phelps were among those who generously supported this initial effort.

Estimated needs were soon fully met: chairs were purchased for the primary room, others were donated out of surplus from nearby homes, song books were selected, and a small organ was bought from Sherman Clay & Company in Oakland. One afternoon early in 1900 a happy group of children gathered for the first time in the new Sunday School, gaily decorated with flowers for the occasion. Among the first arrivals were Elbert, Dorothy and Phyllis Capwell; they were followed in quick succession by the twins, Sadie and Paul Havens, Esther and Herford Sharon, Paul and Johnny Berkenfeld, Girard Richardson, Robert Wing, Colin and Eric Craig and others whose names are out of mind. Some came from quite a distance, and the whole group numbered between thiry and forty. It was a lively lot of close friends, but they evinced unwavering respect toward the gentle-mannered Mrs. Smith and drank in her instruction. The outlet for their high spirits came with the singing. They liked the organ and sometimes stood about it, lustily singing their favorite hymns.

For two years the attendance continued to swell, until the quarters seemed almost inadequate. Then came the sudden death of Mrs. Smith in April, 1902. An impressive memorial service was conducted in the crowded Sunday School on Easter afternoon. Reverend E. E. Baker, pastor of the First Presbyterian Church of which Mrs. Smith had been a member, presided over the ceremonies. Those who knew her had grown to love and respect this lady who so faithfully made the trip up by cable car to greet her little charges on Sunday afternoon. Mrs. Mygatt, grandmother to the Sharons, then assumed leadership, assisted by Mrs. Frances Thomas, who fostered the next Sunday school gatherings in her home. Mrs. Mygatt played the organ and cared for the primary class. But attendance began to drop off. The Sunday band concerts presented a constant distraction, and Mr. Pattiani began turning me from my Sunday duties by driving me in his one-cylinder Cadillac, number "88" in California registration.

Founding of Mowbray Hall . . .

Before her retirement, Mrs. Mygatt commenced a building fund for further church projects and was able to collect $225.00 towards this fund. Major Woof, a Piedmont property owner, contributed an additional hundred dollars to the sum. In 1904 Mr. Henry Mowbray took charge of the Sunday school, which was held in two small rooms at the home of Miss Blair on Vernal Avenue. Many of the old assistants cooperated with him.

In the Fall of 1906 Reverend H. C. Gause took over, the school then meeting in the carriage house of Mrs. A. F. Merriman on Hillside Avenue. The next summer Mr. Mowbray returned and remained until October, 1908. It was largely through his efforts that the matter of securing an appropriate building was again taken up, and a lot was purchased through the courtesy of Mr. and Mrs. Frank C. Havens. Plans for the building were drawn up. The residents of Piedmont responded generously to another appeal for money. Some were interested in a place for neighborhood gatherings, similar to the "village room" in New England; others were equally concerned over having the Sunday school in a permanent place.

Such was the appreciation in which Mr. Mowbray was held that the feeling was unanimous that the building had to be named "Mowbray Hall". Later the Hall was taken over as headquarters for the Piedmont Masonic Lodge.

Establishment of the Community Church (1909) ...

In October, 1909, Reverend John E. Stuchel, a Presbyterian minister, came to Piedmont to organize an inter-denominational church, and services commenced in Mowbray Hall in the following November. In 1910 the new church adopted by-laws under the name Piedmont Church. In the Fall of that year the pastor's wife, Mrs. Helen E. Stuchel, was elected as the first president of the Women's Guild, organized by the women of the church.

In 1913 the church purchased its present site at Mountain and Highland Avenues and incorporated. By this time the Sunday school had outgrown Mowbray Hall, and construction of the present building began, designed by Mr. Farr and decorated by Mr. Ransome Beach. It was completed and dedicated on January 6, 1918. Several troops of Boy Scouts were assigned quarters there, since they had been sponsored by the church. By remodeling and building additional quarters in the basements, they were able, through the aid of a school shack that had been purchased, to manage fairly well until 1940.

During that year Reverend Holland F. Burr was called to the pastorate. Under his diligent ministry all the groups participating in the various services, including the Pi-Chi whose members are of high school age and the Py-Ads which consists of college students, have increased in numbers, so much that additional housing is necessary for providing facilities for more than twice the number contemplated when the original plans were drawn.

From its inception the Community Church has had the good will and support of Piedmont families who are communicants of other churches in East Bay cities, as well as of its own membership.

Boy Scouts in Piedmont ...

The Piedmont Council claims the distinction of having one of the first, if not the first, Scout Troop west of Chicago. Reverend Stuchel, referred to previously as the pastor of the Piedmont Community Church, had endeavored to find a satisfactory and suitable type of organization for the growing boys of Piedmont. Various schemes were tried and discarded. Finally he noticed an article published in *Outlook Magazine* about the Boy Scout organization in America, which was based on the same principles as those of the founder, Baden Powell.

The matter was discussed among the boys and the first organization meeting and camping trip was held in Redwood Canyon on October 10, 1910. The boys hiked from Piedmont with whatever equipment they could manage to scrape together, since there was no official kit at that time. After this initial try hiking trips were held weekly, and it was real hiking with no automobiles to help out. The official Scout Room was in the carriage house on the property of Mrs. Frances M. Thomas, and meetings were usually held there during the winter months. Mr. Stuchel was a man rich in the lore of nature and was an ideal scout-master.

From the start of that Troop boys came in ever increasing numbers to join the organization. They had the staunch backing of General O. F. Long, Adolph Uhl, Robert Tyson, Will Robertson and Wallace Alexander, who guided and gave time and money to the growing project. When Mr. Stuchel left Piedmont to take another church, the movement broke up. It was reorganized again as a Council, the forty-second to be established nationally, and is still in full operation and the holder of numerous national records.

Mr. Wallace Alexander became its first elected president in 1921 and continued as such until 1935. Among the boys who were in that early troop, as far as the records indicate were Leighton McGregor, Fenwick Smith, John C. Hampton, Jr., Charles E. Hill, Jack, Jim, and Todd Oakley, William Tyson, Horace Breed, Alvin and Harry M. Thomas, John Williams, Bernard, Kenneth and Henry Proctor and Arthur McMurray. Many of these have passed away now, but those still living have developed into men who have accomplished outstanding work in the field of business. So far as is known, the only one of the original Troop to have continued with scouting is Harry M. Thomas, who became an Eagle Scout, the holder of the Silver Beaver and President of the Council from 1951 to 1953 inclusive.

For the Piedmont girls there has been established since 1934 a summer retreat, Camp Augusta, situated near Nevada City, California. It was given as a memorial to Mrs. George C. Collins by her daughter, Mrs. Edward W. Ehman (Charlotte Collins). Each year the girls are sent for two weeks and are chosen according to their age groups. The camp, beautifully surrounded by the Sierra Nevadas, is equipped with every convenience for the comfort and safety of the girls.

More About Religions in Piedmont . . .

Aside from the interdenominational church, Piedmont Community Church, the only other sect that has an edifice actually within the boundary of the City that is of Christ Scientist. In 1924 a small group of Christian Scientists, recognizing a need for a Christian Science church in Piedmont, decided to organize a branch of the Mother Church, the First Church of Christ, Scientist, in Boston, Massachusetts. Several progressive steps had been taken since their first home in Masonic Hall, then in Piedmont Community Hall, and finally their own church edifice at Magnolia and Bonita Avenues. This building site was purchased in 1928 and remodeled, decorated, and furnished in 1937, with the first church service being held there, August 1, 1937. The fact that at the dedication ceremonies the church was free from debt was made possible by a grant from the trustees under the Will of Mary Baker Eddy.

Despite the fact that there is no Catholic Church within Piedmont proper, the City's Catholic citizens are served by two churches right on the boundary lines: Saint Leo's Church and Corpus Christi Church. Although in the earliest days the whole of Piedmont, plus some territory further on into the hills, all belonged to the parish of Saint

Interior glympse of *Wildwood*

Frances de Sales with the church at Twenty-First and Grove Streets in Oakland, as the territory became more densely populated, the parish lines were shifted, and now these two newer churches serve the City of Piedmont.

The Ransom-Bridges Private School
for Girls (1912)...

Among the more important institutions of the City was ranked the Ransom-Bridges School. The dream of a private school for girls of this blossoming city came first to Mrs. Oscar Fitzalen Long. Her two small girls, Amy and Sally, were ready to discard the private intructions and join with others in competitive study at a school near to home.

With her efficency and energy Mrs. Long persuaded Miss Margaret Ransom, then an instructor at Miss Anna Head's School in Berkeley, to come to Piedmont. Miss Ransom brought with her Miss Edith Bridges as an assistant. They obtained the recently evacuated Havens house at the corner of Highland Avenue and Hazel Lane. The Havens had lived here before moving to their Wildwood estate. The cost of tuition was high and the admittance requirements had to meet scholastic and social standards of a most exacting character. However, the attendance grew until the great demand made the construction of a permanent building seem advisable. The Wallace Alexanders, with their daughter Martha a student, were deeply concerned in the expansion of the school, and, with the cooperation of other parents, they financed the purchase of the old Booth property at the end of Hazel Lane and the erection of a large, well-planned modern building with accomodations for fifty or more boarders. The classrooms were in low, rambling structures at a short distance from the main house. Miss Ransom and Miss Bridges moved their school into the new quarters during the year 1913. The City of Piedmont felt very proud of this latest venture and accorded it every possible assistance. The attendance soon reached its capacity and the scholastic standing of the institution soon received top rating at both the University of California and Stanford University.

Love of this school is treasured deep within the hearts of many women still living in Piedmont, and hundreds more alumnae members are scattered over the world. It is impossible to do more than touch upon the cultural advantages that this fine school rendered to the entire community.

Unfortunately, since the school depended on private support, the financial crash of 1929 brought in its wake the final destruction of this institution. Now, with its former teachers spread over distant lands, the school itself is disbanded and the building razed.

Miss Wallace's School for Girls ...

Another private school that ranks high in scholastic and social prestige is Miss Wallace's School. For years Miss Wallace was a private tutor in Piedmont, but coaching is only corrective surgery and she felt that a school would provide preventive medicine. In 1925 the little cottage on Mountain Avenue where she held her coaching classes became too small, and she leased a piece of property at Sotello Avenue and Glen Alpine Road and moved up there in late January, 1925. At that time it was such a wild place that it seemed as though it might well have been called "Miss Wallace's Folly". The swimming pool was two feet deep in mud and filth and the only building consisted of a playhouse and a kitchen which had formerly been used for parties; the tennis court was covered with filth. But in the Spring a tiny house was added to the kitchen, and that June the first class graduated under the lovely oaks on the slope of the hill. The two graduates were Ethel Nicolls, daughter of Mr. and Mrs. W. C. Nicolls, and Evelyn Smith, daughter of Mrs Francis M. Smith, the widow of the Borax King who was so closely involved with Frank Havens and his varied ventures.

A few years later, through the generosity of one of the patrons of the school, the present site on Pacific Avenue was purchased, and later still Miss Wallace bought another small house for dormitories, music and art.

The basic tenet upon which Miss Wallace founded her school was that character is essential for education and it follows that a stable character is synonomous with academic standing. To build a sound mind in a sound body, she believed in an outdoor freedom of life. The result was that the girls left the school knowing the difference between right and wrong and in excellent health. The latter fact was the result of ninety-five percent of her work being done out-of-doors, despite weather conditions. A third thing that Miss Wallace found to be true in dealing with children, a truth that the great religious men of the world have always known, was that the younger the child began the better the results. So the school became known, perhaps to its financial disadvantage, as one that welcomed the pre-school child. Long before the Nursery School was widely known, Miss Wallace lectured on the subject in an effort to enthuse parents on its value.

Many well known names have been associated with the school: the James Doles, the Wallace Alexanders, the Stanley Dollars, the James K. Moffitts, and the George Townes are only a few who have helped and have been helped by this little school.

Most of the graduates have gone on to college, and, better still, most of them are happily married. The school is still a thriving insti-tution.

The Public School System of Piedmont has long been an illustrious organization but cannot be given its full share of limelight at present. Suffice it to say that with its five schools of varying levels (1) it does an outstanding community service in educating the young people of our City.

The Piedmont Garden Club . . .

Founded in 1923 by Mrs. C. C. Clay with Mrs. Arthur G. Tasheira as President, the Piedmont Garden Club was accepted in 1926 as a full-fledged member of the Garden Club of America which aims *". . . to stimulate the knowledge and love of gardening among amateurs, to share the advantages of association through conferences and correspon-dence in this country and abroad, to aid in the protection of native plants and birds, to encourage civic planting . . ."*

During the thirty years of the Club's existence, money has been raised through dues, garden tours, flower shows and markets and by individual subscription. Various projects have been civic beautification, Save-the-Redwoods League, National Tribute Grove, Roadside Coun-cil, conservation of national resources and finally teacher training in nature subjects. During the war years activities extended to the plant-ing and beautification of hospital and chapel areas at Camp Roberts, Mather Field, Fort Ord, Camp Knight, Camp Stoneman, Oakland Area Hospital and Treasure Island. In 1943 bi-weekly flower service to the military hospitals was started and continued until 1947.

---

(1) Cf. Appendix V for names of schools and dates of establishment.

Other Civic Organizations . . .

Among the many groups that have been organized and disbanded through the years in Piedmont, the three most important, perhaps, were the Piedmont Musical Club, the Piedmont Men's Club and the city's branch of the Red Cross. Concerning the first, the Musical Club, not much has been recorded, save that it was founded in 1910 by Dr. H. Melville Tenney. (2) The Piedmont Men's Club, formed March 19, 1912, has had almost no recogntion, for its life was of short duration. The prominence of the leaders, however, drew into their social orbit the newcomers to the City, whose votes in the next election would be cast for the Council members supported by the Club. (3) In August, 1914, World War I drew the country into action, and Red Cross services became a necessity. Mrs. Wallace Alexander assumed leadership over the East Bay territory. Invitations went out to leading women from the social ranks of Oakland, Piedmont and Alameda, with meetings scheduled to be held at Mrs. Alexander's home on Sea View Avenue. (4) These women, in cooperation with similar groups, rendered splendid assistance towards the comfort and well-being of the American doughboys in Europe.

Thus, through the many facets of religion, education and society, we see that Piedmont was a leading and moving influence over the rest of the Bay area and was never known to lag behind any of her neighboring sister-cities.

THE HOME OF YESTERYEAR

Childhood Memories of the Piedmont Home . . .

The house is like a very dear friend to me, even when emptied of those who have kept it ever overflowing with life and movement and inconsequential chatter. I knew it was there, solid, comfortable and comforting, giving an atmosphere of welcome to all who entered the old front door, down through several generations of family and friends.

When in 1879 our Victorian style English Cottage commenced to take shape, it was located in the center of the Craig six-acre tract, with the front entrance facing the West towards Vernal Avenue. The

---

(2) Cf. Appendix VI for officers and committee members of the club.
(3) Cf. Appendix VII for the men at the original meeting of this club.
(4) Cf. Appendix VIII for some of these early members.

pepper-tree shaded driveway leading up into the grounds has been gone for many years, and the gravel road which circled around the house between lawns and flower beds and out to the stable-yard beyond is now but a memory. Everything seemed so beautiful then. We children made pets of all the animals on the place. Our carriage horse had almost human intelligence, and there was a spirited buckskin pony to ride. Life was simple. Happiness and play far outweighed the occasional noisy quarrels and their subsequent corrections behind closed doors.

So the years rolled on. My own marriage and those of Roy and Margery took us to new duties, and vacant rooms were left behind. It was not long until Jessie, Colin and Eric each found interests elsewhere. Taxes were looming on this acreage right in "the Heart of Piedmont", and our parents were aging along with the house. No longer did anyone love to care for those three marble mantles and their coal-burning fire-places, nor the big kitchen range, not to mention the little wood stoves that had to be kindled on a cold winter morn. Those days were fast flitting away.

Changes Come to the Craig Home ...

But the sturdy old house caught again the spirit of youth and accepted upheaval and modernization. Prying it loose from its brick foundation in 1912, the mallets and picks of Henderson's movers came knocking away the redwood supports, as they pushed under the heavy wooden rollers. Slowly and skillfully, amid creaks and groans, the huge hulk was dragged away from its anchorage. A windlass and rope and a blindfolded horse pulled the gabled structure backward, down into the lower corner of the orchard where the unsightly rear, so left when rooms were demolished, would be hidden from view. The family moved with it, and their hearts were wrenched far more than the framework itself or the chimneys which escaped without even a crack.

The charm and personality that had radiated from the dear home seemed to disappear, as it was tagged with a number and became just one of a row on the street.

Grading Troubles ...

When the plows and scrapers commenced their work along the new artery the uprooted house began to loom higher and higher above the deepening grade. Surveyors had failed to figure the depth necessary for making a proper level at its Mountain Avenue intersection. The family were greatly disturbed, for a flight of steps forced undue hardships on the elders who had visioned an easier entrance. But soon a fresh garden began to take shape with new plants and those brought from the older yard, including two large camellia bushes, which afforded in season that familiar flower in the button-hole of Father's coat lapel. The choice bloom was frequently passed on to some lady, ere San Francisco was reached. An astracan apple, a strawberry peach and an apricot tree, along with some berries, helped give a flavor of home to a small back yard. Yet the old time life within had suffered the inevitable family disintegration and found its return to a happier mood only when the voices of grandchildren later brought sounds of merry laughter within its walls. As a grandmother lives again with each generation so does an old house.

Sorrows Come to the Family Circle ...

A shadow of sorrow had accompanied the home as it slid over the ground to its new location. Colin, the pride of the family, an athlete, tall and ambitious, had, in a race with his friend Harold Fagan, experienced a lung hemorrhage. Then only twenty years old he bravely accepted every known care, but in 1916 the physical strength ebbed away from the brother we so loved. The war was raging in all its fury, and mental unrest seemed to be sweeping over the entire world. At the end of the struggle came the "flu" epidemic, which, during the cold days of early January, 1919, gripped our dear Mother. It turned into pneumonia and the devoted skill of Doctor Liliencrantz could not save her. The loss of her warm personality chilled the heart of the home.

Then came a year of patient existence for Father with only a housekeeper to care for his needs. He looked forward eagerly to the day when the Pattiani family could arrange to take over the Craig Avenue property for remodeling and another renovation. Until that date did arrive, the weakened grandfather enjoyed a few weeks with us in Alameda. By early November, 1920, all was in readiness for the return to his own freshened room in the home he loved, where he could hear the voices of grandchildren echoing within its walls.

The move was safely made and a brief week of contentment followed, as each day he sat in the front room listening to a few favorite tunes on the piano. But on the morning of Armistice Day Father suddenly weakened, and at the very moment when the clock in his room began to strike eleven, the brave spirit passed on into the keeping of a merciful God. The solemn tones of a Scout Band, playing before the Piedmont Memorial, floated into the open windows as my husband and Doctor Crosby led me from the bedside. Shortly thereafter, we heard the bugler sounding Taps, an unsought tribute to a noble soul.

Since Father had become a Mason before leaving New Zealand, it seemed fitting to have the simple services in our home conducted under the auspices of Masonic ritual. But his religious faith embraced all creeds and was expressed in his kindness to all mankind.

Testimonial Given by the Council ...

Among the many tributes received by the Craig family came the following resolution from the Piedmont City Council:

"The attention of the Board having been called to the recent death of Mr. Hugh Craig, formerly a Trustee of this City, the following resolution was unanimously adopted:

Resolved: That in the death of Hugh Craig this city has lost one of its leading citizens and foremost workers for the up-building of an independent and competent city government; that his services in the days of the formation of the city, and in the formulation of its policies as a municipality have left their stamp upon its history for all time; that his courage and aggressiveness in asserting and defending what he considered true civic policies are worthy of emulation; that as the first President of the Board he gave his time and abilities unstintedly for several years, during which time many important ordinances, fixing the future status of and character of the City as a strictly residential municipality were adopted; that now that he has passed beyond, we, as the present representatives of the City, deem it our privilege as well as duty to inscribe upon our records this testimonial to his memory.

"Resolved further: That a certified copy of this resolution be delivered by the City Clerk to the family of Mr. Craig."

Another Generation in the Old House ...

At the opening of the expanding era of the twenties numerous clubs and social groups were formed. Their activities brought Piedmont into its season of "full bloom."

The old house felt a touch of this magic as it stood proudly high

Piedmonters going home

above the street, minus most of its original "ginger-bread" trimmings. It glistened anew with paint of a fresh green color that blended into the background of trees. Young life was again filling the high-ceiling rooms with music and dancing and joy, though plenty of hours were spent at good hard study and fulfilling of school reading requirements.

The years sped along. After graduation from Ransom's, our Elizabeth was kept busy with four more years down at the "Stanford Farm". Her return to home and family lasted only a few months. On May 1, 1928, another wedding day came to the old house, when a "Zeta Psi" Stanfordite, Edward Athelstane Howard, gaily led his bride down the front steps and off to a new life and home, far away near the Pasadena foothills.

During the prosperous years of the rise into '29, the sturdy home had its festivities and continued to hold a modest, steady place on the Avenue. From it a business man hastened off each morning, like his neighbors, to catch a San Francisco train, and Ynez went across the Park to Ransom School. How often are the happy periods of life followed by more troubled years! In the early thirties the widespread financial tensions caused the resistance of many executives to give way, and my own good husband went with a sudden heart attack in June of 1932. The old house had lost another master who appreciated its stability and tradition. Under the spread of the wide-eaved roof came kind friends, helping Ynez and me to gain fresh courage and serenity. Soon again youthful voices with laughter and music rang through the rooms.

Eight busy years flitted by, and then another wedding in the Community Church across the way. The reception which followed filled the dear old home with flowers, friends and sentimental reminders. The hour arrived when Donald Houston Graham, Jr., joyously led my Ynez down the front steps and off to their dear "Fairy-land Dream."

Learning to let go is not easy but is necessary in this ever changing repetition of life moving forward. It left me in blank silence as the shadows seemed to fall within the lonely rooms. However, within less than a week a realtor came knocking at the door, looking for a house to lease for a New York couple with three little children, a butler, a cook and a nursemaid. So the William Bowlton Bates family became my tenants for a period of nearly six years, and they loved the old cottage with its many bedrooms and bathrooms.

The Beloved Home Passes to Other Hands . . .

After their departure I felt no inclination to assume again the up-keep. Commercialism was exerting a forceful sway and telling the "Home Sweet Home" that it must now accept new ownership. So with a sad heart and a mist of tears, I signed the deed that gave it over to contractor Hansen. With his family living and working there for several years, he spent many thousands in modernizing the well built structure. In a fresh coating of cream paint, its appearance and size intrigued the J. Stanley Stephens, a numerous clan, into becoming the next owners. They have enjoyed the place and enhanced its charm to moderns by developing the facilities of outdoor living in the sheltered, rear garden, but necessity is now calling the family else-where. In due time other boys and girls will be skipping down the steps from 55 Craig and away to their classes at the several Piedmont Schools.

This house, built so long ago with redwood timbers throughout, has refused to accept any nesting termites which have no taste for that flavored wood. Preserved, too, it has been from the sparks of consuming fire, which in the years gone by destroyed its contemporary neighbors. What the Redwoods are to California, the oldest of all trees, this stalwart house is to all others in the Piedmont of today, and only the distant future will unfold the final destiny of a beloved home.

STROLLING

A Brief Forward to Strolling . . .

An imaginative stroll along the winding paths and roads of Piedmont makes me long to linger before the gardens and homes that were here established during the late nineteenth and early twentieth centuries. I would like to mention the names of all those who have come to reside within the confines of our Queen City. However, it is necessary to refrain from such an attempt, lest an unwitting omission cause offense. Many of those who have been mentioned have already left the scene of action. Others, of younger years, are now occupying some of those homes and expressing their personalities and ideas in words and deeds. The future of Piedmont remains in their hands; it is the people themselves and the way they conform to an environment that makes up the history of a place.

Development of the Blair Fields
by the Realty Syndicate ...

A section of Piedmont which was most notably developed during the period of 1910 to 1914 extended over what had been the Blair fields at one time, but that was before the Realty Syndicate acquired control. Frank C. Havens and his brother-in-law, Harmon Bell, who was an attorney, assisted by a realtor, E. A. Heron, were the principals in the organization and naturally were most anxious to sell lots nearest to their new electric car line.

The names of prominent Oakland citizens soon appeared upon the lists of new Piedmont taxpayers, and it might make interesting reading were an accurate and complete compilation possible. Friends and school companions came in groups, largely from neighborhoods in the vicinities of the Congregational and Presbyterian churches. Reverend Charles K. Brown, pastor of the Congregational Church, purchased lots on Blair and Bonita Avenues but did not build upon them. In 1908 he sold the corner to the William O. Morgans, who have since contributed so generously to the constructive advancement of the City. Mrs. Morgan is a member of the Vance family, which has extensive lumber interest in the Redwood regions of northern California. The Vances have recently donated a sizeable tract of this magnificent timber land as an addition to the large public domain.

Construction Towards Moraga Avenue ...

In this year of 1910 there were but 210 names on the City taxpayer rolls, and construction of new homes spread towards the Moraga Avenue district. The Keating and also the Broadwater families located in this area. Other new settlers included the families of Lowell Hardy, Vernon Waldron, George W. McNear, Jr., Wallace W. Everett, Edward Prather and Will de Fremery. De Fremery was a nephew of the pioneer James de Fremery who came to San Francisco in 1849. His many descendants in the Bay region are carrying on the distinguished name of their forebear, and a great-grandchild now residing in Piedmont is Mrs. Kent Sawyer of Wildwood Gardens.

Fronting on Hillside and near Blair Avenue was the home of Mrs. Constance Miles Overton and the late Major Winfield Scott Overton, USA. During their decade of life there, the three young daughters were students at the Ransom-Bridges School, and this house was an important center in the fostering of both cultural and welfare interests about the East Bay region. The spacious rooms were often opened to benefits for charitable causes by the generous hostess, who showed her guests the artistic gardens filled with rare plants and shrubs.

Major Overton's name may be of particular interest to Californians who served in World War I. When he was recalled to active service, he was made commander of the students' army training corps at the University of California. At the close of that war he organized the Reserve Officers Training Corps units in all the San Francisco schools. Major Overton is buried in Arlington National Cemetery, Washington, D. C.

Very near neighbors to the Overtons and of contemporary date were the Oliver Ellsworths and their young daughter who was also a Ransom girl. Until the sudden death of Mr. Ellsworth in 1936, the dignified house at Bonita and Highland Avenues had been his residence during the twenty-five years of devoted service as our Mayor.

On Dracina Avenue, opposite the Park of that name, lived the late Mr. Walter Brann and his wife and daughters. Mr. Brann served as a member of the Piedmont Board of Education during the difficult years when buildings were in the process of construction and a good consulting lawyer's advice very important. Wandering up to Bonita Avenue, we find one of the earliest houses, designed by Harry St. L. Farr who had married Blanche Sharon. They lived here with their two small sons, until they moved up to a newer home on Sharon Avenue. The place on Bonita was then purchased by the late Mr. and Mrs. Van Horn Cooley. A lovely wedding was celebrated in this house when Eric Kenneth Craig, my brother, claimed his University classmate, Esther Cooley, as his bride, July 3, 1912.

Homes Built near Old Peralta Homestead Site ...

And next door is Mrs. Samuel Taylor still retaining the home and memory of her late husband, who took an active part in civic affairs during many of the formative years of the municipality. Among others who located near the new electric line were the twins, Addie and Carrie Gorrill, sisters of attorney Will Gorrill. The sisters were prominent in University life during the Gay Nineties.

Then on Ramona Avenue is found Warren P. Myers, with his wife Ann and their son. Ann Myers was one of the many children of the well-known McElrath family whose estate once comprised the entire property now occupied by the Children's Hospital of the East Bay. This section was the land bordering on Temescal Creek, and it had been the location of the Vicente Peralta homestead.

Still strolling in this location, we pass the Monticello residence of a senior citizen, Mr. C. U. Martin, from whose home there is an expansive view of the Bay. Near neighbors on Lorita Avenue is the house of Mr. Lawrence Moore, who served so faithfully for such a length of time as a member of the City Council and again as our Mayor.

Rounding the curves out Park Way, we come upon the home of the Charles A. Strongs. Captain Strong has been especially honored for his staunch support and devotion to the Boy Scouts.

As lots were gradually sold, building continued to ornament this part of the community where many more good citizens have come to reside. However, interest in real estate began to shift towards the Springs Park at about the time that Blair Avenue was paved east from Highland and Hardwick was cut through to Oakland Avenue. An enthusiastic young couple braved the wide fields and built one of the first houses on this short street. Jessie Fox, daughter of the well konwn Lake District family of that name, had been married to young Edson Adams, a nephew of the late Edson F. Adams. With their son Frank and daughter they became active in the social and civic affairs of the new city. Mrs. Adams is among the lamentably few of those early citizens whose friends can still find her in the original home. Frank Adams now lives up on Scenic Avenue with his wife and growing family about him.

Hardwick Avenue Properties . . .

On the east side of Hardwick, in the center of the block stood the house built in the late seventies by the Bowman-Wright families. It was later purchased and occupied for years by Mrs. Frank Demming and her two daughters. They lived a rather secluded life within the big house, which was circled by a curving driveway amid trees and heavy foliage.

Changes and the death of Mrs. Demming caused the main portion of this estate to be sold. It was purchased and remodeled by Mrs. Ruth Dunham Langdon and Colonel Langdon. With their large family, they enjoyed it for a number of years, until country life over in Marin induced them to dispose of this place. After being idle for a lengthy period, wreckers and realtors finally transformed the property into a modern subdivision. Miss Inez Demming still retains ownership to the north corner at Blair and Hardwick.

Ransome-Bridges School—June 8, 1923

Some years ago Mrs. George Marwedell and her daughter moved into this Blair neighborhood. As one of the lovely Taft sisters, her name and that of her late husband, are reminders of successful pioneer ancestors. Lingering here for a moment longer, one can be certain of receiving a cordial greeting from Mrs. Kendall Morgan, Maud Bell Hampton as her many friends have long known her. She stems from an old time Oakland family, belonging to that Market Street contingent.

Final Fate of Worcester Knoll ...

Climbing up to what was once known as Worcester Knoll, we are again reminded of that spirited genius, Jack London, to whom after his two years of residence here we were forced to bid farewell.

Then for a time this hill was deserted, until a family from San Francisco moved over into these bungalows, Mr. and Mrs. James J. Fagan, with their sons Harold and Paul and a baby sister. The fame of the health-giving climate seemed to have been the inducement which drew them across the Bay. They were a lively addition to the neighborhood tribe that frequented our tennis court and raided the orchard. Games often turned into riots before the boys made off to other fields of action. There were no Scout troops or constructive diversions to hold the young people from the attractions offered in the city below.

After the Fagans departed that choice piece of acreage was acquired by Mr. Oscar Sutro, and on it he built a beautiful home for his family where, for some years, radiated the gaieties of that period. When death overtook the head of the family, their migration to San Francisco followed, and the well known name of Sutro was removed from the door plate.

Only for a few months was this stately mansion devoid of occupants, when it re-opened its doors to Mr. and Mrs. Mark Requa with their two daughters and son Lawrence. They lived here only while their new home up on Mountain Avenue was under construction. So the "Worcester Knoll" again awaited the arrival of others who would love the panoramic view it had to offer. Soon they came; Dr. Sharpstein and his family from Alameda, remaining as residents for a goodly number of years.

Before turning down on to Oakland Avenue, we reach the corner where Pacific touches and pause for breath and a few background notes. The lower portion of this street became a connecting link between Mountain and the upper end of Oakland Avenue soon after

Dingee made this extension and started selling lots at his famous Auction. In the eucalyptus forest on the hillside to the east, stood the new home, recently built by Harmon Bell. A son Traylor and wife Helen, daughter of the pioneers, Mr. and Mrs. Quincy Chase, now live on this block of Oakland Avenue, as do Mr. and Mrs. Houghton Sawyer, a distinguished name among local architects.

A neighborly stop must be made along here to knock at the door of Captain Horace Strother, where friends are welcomed as he reminisces of earlier days. Both Captain and Mrs. Strother will be numbered among those devoted citizens who aided in church and civic developments.

Somewhat belatedly has Caroline Palmentier Snowden finally brought to this avenue a reminder of an old and honored family who just missed building their Linda Vista home within the boundary lines of Piedmont. William G. Palmentier drew many depositors from this hill section to the new red brick bank at Fourteenth and Broadway Streets, of which he was the first President.

Mountain Avenue and Doctor Crosby . . .

The first house that was constructed well up on the Mountain Avenue trail was long the home of Mrs. Florence Wing, who had entered it as a bride in 1878. Her son Robert and his family had followed interests calling them far from Piedmont. Failing health made it impossible for her to remain there alone.

With closed doors and shuttered windows the old home kept vigil over the neglected garden for a time, until Dr. Daniel Crosby and his wife Agnes entered its empty rooms. The wide expanse of Bay and hills enthralled them, and soon the property was theirs. With some interior remodeling they made ready to welcome the family. A rare collection of antiques which adorned the residence was an inheritance belonging to Mrs. Crosby, who received them from the late President James Buchanan to whom she was related.

Enough land for a large yard around the house was retained, while surveys were made of the remaining property which was sold off as home sites. The Ernest Mendenhalls were among the first to build on that Mountain Avenue frontage, and adjoining them is a more recently planned home now occupied by Mr. and Mrs. Dwayne Young (Allene Edoff). The wife is the daughter of an old Oakland family.

Lifetime of Service ...

The gnarled old shade trees in the quiet, secluded garden offered a rest from the hours of work for the busy doctor with his generous heart. Few could know of the countless acts by which he tried to lighten the burdens of his patients. An infectious laugh or the clever twist of a phrase would permit them to see the funny side of their malady, allowing their mental and physical healing to progress.

A lifetime of service in the East Bay made for "Dan Crosby" a host of devoted friends. His automobile sped its way up and down Mountain Avenue and into Craig Avenue at all hours of the day and the night. His years of practice included that period of optimistic and prosperous climb to the eagerly awaited era of perpetual prosperity. Piedmont re-echoed to these gay times, and this home with vivacious Agnes Crosby as hostess radiated the prevailing spirit of hospitality. Closely associated with Mrs. Crosby was Mrs. Arthur Tashiera (Helen Garthwaite), whose Colonial style home on Muir Avenue was ever a center of activity.

The years of depression crashed down and put an abrupt end to this tinselled period. The good doctor worked even harder than before, as calls of distress came with increasing urgency to his home and office. At all hours they were answered, needy and wealthy alike, according to the individual necessity.

An untimely death called this beloved doctor to long sought rest, leaving all who knew him the memory of a magnificent man. The daughter Virginia, now Mrs. Joseph S. Bancroft, occupied the old home for a time, and young Daniel Crosby Bancroft carries on the honored name of his grandfather.

Though a comparatively late comer to the hill city, Dr. Crosby took under his protection and care the lonely, frail and poverty-stricken daughter of Piedmont's pioneer citizen, Walter Blair. Through the artful manueverings of several persons of promenince and wealth, the rightful inheritance of Mabel Blair Squires went into the pocket of others. Thanks to the late Dr. Crosby's earlier ministrations, she was cared for at the County Hospital near Hayward, where she lay for years a hopeless and helpless invalid.

Where is Piedmont's loyalty to its own?

Pacific Avenue District ...

The continuation of Pacific appears about the year 1909, coinciding with the cutting and clearing of H. C. Hagars' eucalyptus groves which was to the south of Bell forest. A graded artery was made to connect with the upper end of Mountain Avenue, thus making saleable the Hagars' hillside acres. Probably this trail originally acquired the name "Pacific" because of the views to be had from its every homesite toward the ocean.

Building, however, progressed slowly, for the grades were quite a problem. Horses, of course, did the hauling in those days before the mechanized truck. The first houses built up on these heights were for the Hagar daughters, Mrs. Helen Moore and Mrs. Louise Tallman.

By 1914 another couple from the Oakland contingent of established families, Mr. and Mrs. Frederick Potter, selected a scenic Pacific Avenue site. Mrs. Elizabeth Potter was a daughter of the late George E. Grays, long members of the Market Street group. She was active in library and editorial work and is the author of the much read book, *The Skyline of San Francisco.* Her sister Mabel, known to Piedmonters as Mrs. Thomas Mitchell Potter, devoted a lifetime of brilliant executive service to worthwhile activities throughout the East Bay. She had contributed her very youthful services to the First Presbyterian Church Sunday school. Later she was President of the Ebell Club for several consecutive years. As an alumnae of Mills College Mrs. Potter remained active in the progress of that institution. A memorial is being prepared in the new library to honor this outstanding citizen. After her sudden death in Piedmont the Council passed upon its records an official note of appreciation for her years of constructive service.

More on Pacific Heights . . .

While still up on these Pacific heights, we discover another home belonging to those who braved out the rough woods and barren fields: Mrs. Omar Cox and her daughter, both very active in community welfare projects. Here, too, is the unique private school that Miss Mary Wallace has successfully conducted for so long.

Turning down the curving Avenue, a momentary stop is made before the home of the late Harry W. Jones, perhaps known to more of the young people than any other single person in Piedmont. The Board of Education selected Mr. Jones as Principal of the High School at the time of its opening in August, 1921. He served continuously in this capacity over a period of twenty-seven years, while also acquiring the title of Superintendent of the City Schools.

Across the street at the corner of Pacific and Craig are the Laidleys and Mary Ella, now Mrs. Lenahan, who have clung to this neighborhood for over thirty years. Another home on the curve of this three-way intersection recalls to mind the names of Captain and Mrs. Dunwoody. They seemed constantly fearful of accidents as the automobiles came tearing through the streets. Holding tenaciously to old-time tradition is Campbell Carmine, a nephew of Mrs. Dunwoody. He now resides in this same home with his wife and two lovely daughters.

Development in the Heart of Piedmont . . .

A descendant of the famed Colonel John C. Hayes, noted earlier in these pages, now carries on his grandfather's name on Craig Avenue. The younger Jack Hayes family lived for many years on Mountain Avenue, and they possess a background in local history that ties in with the heart of Piedmont. Writing of this spot brings happy memories of "the Hills of Home" and the names of a few more neighbors who are still living in their original homes: Mrs. Chick, Mrs. Freudenthal and Mrs. George Davis. Then there is the *Quida Morada* home, designed by the late Miss Juliet Alexander. It now belongs to the Earl Fishers, who must be enjoying the picturesque Hawaiian patio and gardens. At the southeast corner the attractive Colonial cottage remains as a reminder of Louis Breuner who planned and built it. They have since moved elsewhere.

Crossing Highland Avenue, we remember the Oliver Kehrline family who once lived in the big house at the corner of Oakland and Hillside Avenues. But it has been occupied for a long time by the Ward Dawsons. On the other half of the block is the home that belonged first to the Channels and then was taken over by the Butters, from whom the Sisters of the Holy Family purchased it. These homes lent a distinction to the upper side of the street. The opposite side was the site of the English style home of the R. W. Gorrills and their daughter Grace (now Mrs. W. W. Potter). They had a wide outlook over the terrain beneath.

A residence of similar architecture was constructed for Willard Williamson and his wife Paula. She was one of the stunning Rued daughters, from the old Oakland family on Linden Street. But Willard himself is connected with this story, for he was the sole merry look among us in that first Piedmont School picture, taken in 1886. But a suburban life could not hold the family permanently, and they soon moved to San Francisco.

A square, three-story structure on the corner of Magnolia Avenue was planned and built by Mr. and Mrs. A. Lowndes Scott before 1900. Sorrows came to this family, however, and neighbors reluctantly bid farewell to the widow and her son. One of the stateliest homes in Piedmont still stands on this block. The name of James K. Lockhead, President of the American Trust Company, is proudly displayed upon the mailbox. The Colonial pillars are reminders of the Barracloughs who originally built the house in the late nineties. The building changed owners when the widow was married to the well known and popular Ralph Phelps.

Some Glamor Found to Be Indelible . . .

The gradual progression of the population up to higher lands proved the lasting quality of glamour of the Hillside Avenue district. Other sections might be featured and their roads congested by truck-loads of building materials, but here existed a freedom from noise and traffic, and a peaceful quiet still pervades its atmosphere. So the people we knew have come and gone, and now Kinney Block is a playground belonging to all the citizens.

Wandering on past the Civic Center until we reach the intersection of Highland and Mountain Avenues, memory recalls Mr. McGregor, the architect and contractor, who lives quietly with his family at the corner. During those years when the fields were slowly being given the status of city lots, he possessed the courage and foresight to build num-erous homes in this central district, thus hastening its development.

A few steps beyond this and just opposite the Park is the peaceful home of Mrs. Powell, a gentle wife and mother, who has been always ready with time, energy and support for the various activities connected with the church and general welfare of the town.

The prestige of Highland Avenue was further enhanced by the erec-tion of a dignified home overlooking the side entrance and lawns of the Park. Upon its completion Mr. and Mrs. Thomas Cushing (the former Mrs. Joseph Ghirardelli) moved in. The wife continued to draw around her the connections of the numerous Ghirardelli clan who definitely liked to reside in Piedmont. Her daughter Carmen became the wife of George W. Baker, Jr., and their home was a gather-ing place for friends in the Crocker tract neighborhood, until their recent move to San Francisco.

With its wide frontage on the curve into Sierra stands the home built by the Clinton Walkers long ago. The family is now grown and broadly scattered, so Mrs. Walker enjoys a suburban life elsewhere. The wide lawns of the Allen Chickering place come next on our meanderings, and we remember that the joyous occasion of a Golden Wedding anniversary has recently been celebrated there.

Then there is the lovely English style home just beyond the Chickerings, built soon after this tract was opened by Dr. and Mrs. Murray Johnson. Here they lived for several years, until the death of Miss Playter, a sister of the wife's, when they moved into her vacant home on Capetown Avenue. They sold the Sierra Avenue place to the Jack Okell family, to whom it afforded great happiness. The attractive Carlisle domicile is observed as we continue around the curve. It is approached by a gravel driveway, bordered by artistically placed rocks and shrubs and a garden fashioned after nature's own designs.

Across the way is the residence of Mrs. Gilbert Graham and her late husband the doctor. They enjoyed it for many years and have developed a valuable and varied collection of trees and rare shrubs.

Continuing Along Sierra ...

The large, rectangular house on the corner once claimed as its owner the fine old gentleman, Captain Ernest Houdlette, a notable figure in San Francisco's Merchant Exchange. His sons and their families live on Mountain Avenue and are proud citizens of Piedmont.

A flavor of old Dutch ancestry is indicated at the D. Pysel threshold, also located on Sierra. Their European heritage of hospitality has been lavished upon friends and neighbors over the years. Fronting on Sheridan and opposite the end of Sierra is the residence of the late Mrs. Charles F. Houghton who came here from Oakland's once fashionable Lake district. She always recalled pleasant memories to old-timers. A daughter, Mrs. Ruth Hall, still occupies the family residence.

A few steps further in an easterly direction comes a place long famous for its hospitality: the home of the late Judge Everett Brown and his wife. His sister, Miss Annie Florence Brown, was an outstanding citizen of the entire East Bay; although not actually a resident of Piedmont, she was a frequent visitor at the Judge's home. Continuing along from the Browns, we arrive at the house of Mr. and Mrs. Bertram York who were from old pioneer stock. Mrs. York was a daughter of the notable Sadler family of Alameda. The Harvey Lyons were neighbors on this block for years but have since moved out to

Mrs. Wallace Alexander's Red Cross Unit

the Lafayette countryside. Just beyond these homes we see the Colonial structure belonging to Mrs. Eldridge Green. Her love of flowers, particularly those of wild varieties, is displayed in a garden of unusual charm.

Walking on Sheridan Avenue ...

Across Sheridan Avenue at its intersection with Lincoln stands the large house once owned by the Jesse T. Blackallers, whose son and three daughters attended the Piedmont schools during the twenties and thirties. Next door lives a gentleman familiar in banking circles across the Bay, but in this residential town he is more outstanding as the agreeable bachelor, C. Nelson Hackett. Further up the street, where it meets Crocker, is found the pleasant home of Mr. and Mrs. Albert C. Rowe, both of whom radiate generosity and kindness and who have been leaders in local activities, along with their fine sons.

On the other side of the street is the Hart Wilcox residence where three lovely daughters have grown from infancy to the day when they left as joyous young brides. Just beyond the Wilcox gardens were those of the late Miss Jane Rawlings, who had scores of good friends and was active on the Ladies' Relief Board and on other charitable benefits.

A little further up this street is the lovely home where the George Chase family have long held sway. The latch-string is always up for the three married daughters and their numerous grandchildren. On the corner opposite are the Herman Nichols, mentioned previously as having selected that site upon the wild fields of the Crocker tract only moments before the Wallace Alexanders laid their choice upon precisely the same spot.

Meandering Along King Avenue ...

At Number Six, King Avenue, is the large and well seasoned home that ties the Ghirardelli name with that of John Welby Dinsmore. This gentleman served as Mayor of Piedmont (1947) and carried on with the traditional acumen and tact of his own family and that of the clan of his wife Elva, daughter of the late Mrs. Louis Ghirardelli. This notable lady long reigned as social mistress of the home she designed.

In these long-forgotten days when vacant lots were numerable on King Avenue, Mr. and Mrs. William Ede came to pioneer and build themselves a stately home on the upper side of the new street. Here they lived with their sons and entertained for quite a period of time.

As the years went on, Mrs. Ede began to wish for a less pretentious home. Soon the large place was sold and a new one constructed on the corner of Highland and Sierra Avenues.

Mr. and Mrs. Edwin Oliver with their three lively sons and daughter found the Ede house quite to their liking and snapped it up. After making several changes and improvements, the Olivers moved in and created here an outstanding center for both the elder friends and younger people of various ages. The large ballroom on the lower floor was made available for dancing classes and for the first Piedmont assemblies. Mrs. Oliver was nominated as the first presiding patroness over these groups. These were invitational affairs, and few teenagers went around unchaperoned in this well supervised group. The years sped on, and one evening in the flower bedecked home Mr. Oliver gave his only daughter Roberta in marriage to the fine young man, Frederick L. Greenlee. A happy home next door for this couple now echoes with the voices of grandchildren who, when intermingled with those of their many cousins, recall in the Oliver halls the merriment of a former generation.

More About Crocker Tract Subdivisions . . .

Across King Avenue towards the south comes a park-like garden with inviting paths and stepping stones to lure the visitor into a walk down to the Crocker Avenue gateway below. From a spacious Colonial home surrounded by this colorful garden, Mr. and Mrs. Herbert Hall and their family have dispensed hospitality over many long years. The Children's Hospital branches are frequently welcomed into this lovely place on those days in the Spring when Benefit Teas are the vogue.

Development over this portion of the Crocker tract began to expand during the early years of the 1920's. Particularly was this true after the death of Mr. and Mrs. Richardson, when the son Girard had the home wrecked and an avenue named for the family cut through the property, thus making more building sites available.

On a sunny Caperton Avenue corner stands a large house of English architecture, where the Maxwell Taft family lived for many years. That honored and familiar name brings to mind Oakland's one-time leading dry goods store, Taft and Pennoyer's. The firm established its first place of business on Broadway between Thirteenth and Fourteenth Streets, later moving to their new building at Clay, between Fourteenth and Fifteenth Streets. Inside, choice silks and satins were sometimes displayed over the counter by Mr. Taft himself, especially when unsurpassed quality was requested by his friends, Mrs. Requa or Mrs. Wheaton and others too numerous to mention.

Before leaving the Caperton Avenue neighborhood, it may be of interest to recall the late Judge Ergo Majors and his wife. She still resides here among her collection of treasures gathered on travels to foreign lands. More than a few automobile drivers who forgot the speed limit rules may remember Piedmont's court room, where both a lecture was delivered and a fine imposed upon the culprits by Judge Majors.

The Bliss Menage . . .

Turning south again and on to Crocker Avenue, we come upon the Bliss home. A San Franciscan and his wife had found here, while the wild flowers were still coloring every vacant lot, a location to their liking and an architect to design a house for them. By 1914 a large and well proportioned structure on this Avenue was ready to welcome Mr. and Mrs. Charles Tobey Bliss to the hill town.

Mrs. Bliss was the daughter of the late Captain and Mrs. J. N. Knowles of Jackson Street, an outstanding pioneer family of Oakland. Mr. "Bud" Bliss, as he was familiarly known, belongs to the clan of that name who owned such extensive lumber in Nevada and near Lake Tahoe. Their Truckee River Railroad and Tahoe Tavern have long been internationally famous.

In 1934 Elizabeth Bliss and J. Paul St. Sure were married, and they now live with their two daughters in a pretty home closer to the hills.

Wildwood Avenue Wanderings . . .

Roaming south across the car tracks to Wildwood Avenue, we observe the handsome grilled iron gates standing open before a clear pool surrounded by a circular driveway leading to the Bert Scott front door. The family came from Alameda in 1918 and selected the newly built house for its Tudor-English design and the superb architecture of Albert Farr. Sons Kenneth and "Bud" and daughter Kathleen have now gone off to homes of their own and return only as visitors to the parental roof.

The much-heralded airplane, the Hall-Scott Motor, famed for its excellence in World War I, was invented and made available through the clever minds and business sagacity of these two Piedmont men. Mr.

Hall lived for many years in the large and formal house on Muir Avenue.

Momentarily diverting our stroll off Wildwood and through the pillared gateway into Woodland Way, one is reminded of the lively young people who grew up in this home at the corner leading into Wildwood Gardens. They carried on the name of a distinguished grandfather, the founder of Hills Brothers Coffee.

Councilman Fairchild . . .

The broad, curving property immediately adjacent to this has been the home of the Fairchilds for the past twenty years, and here must we give pause to speak of one of Piedmont's esteemed Councilmen.

After a periodic slump in building activities during the first years of the 1920's, the tide again flowed, Piedmont was once more reflecting the prosperity that was sweeping the country from coast to coast. Young men holding executive positions were looking with favor upon the "exclusive city", as a place to live and to rear their children. The trend of the wealthier population was away from congested areas and Piedmont offered numerous advantages. The Wildwood Garden district, surrounding Mrs. Frank C. Havens East Indian palace, joined the list of estates that were being divided up into smaller holdings.

Joseph S. Fairchild and his young wife, Alberta Clark (daughter of the A. V. Clarks of Alameda and owners of the California Pottery Company), purchased a lovely home just inside the Garden gateway. There they lived for twenty years and reared their two daughters amid these ideal surroundings. Special mention is due Mr. Fairchild for the devoted interest he expended in his management of civic affairs. For ten years he was chosen by the electorate to serve on the City Council, at each election winning a majority vote over the entrenched forces of the Old Guard. But in 1947 as his turn came for the elevation to the Mayor's chair, everyone realized that Joseph Fairchild had won the confidence and respect of his former opponents. He was truly a man of independent thinking, unbiased by any political control, and upright and honest in his judgments.

Recognition of ability has now taken Mr. Fairchild to the Eastern Coast. There he has assumed the position of Vice-President of the Board of the United States Envelope Company, with which firm he was associated here in California. In all his varied pursuits Mr. Fairchild has demonstrated a spirit of cooperation and the strong hand of leadership.

Oak-Lined Woodland Way . . .

Under the spreading oaks along this shaded Woodland Way is a sweet garden of begonias and ferns with a pathway leading to an attractive home now owned by Mr. and Mrs. Montgomery Haslett. The husband came from Alameda where the Haslett family has rated social prestige over several generations. Winding around this curving drive, we pass the cosy menage of the Frank Edoffs, scion of an East Bay family of noteworthy accomplishment.

Then we approach the broad expanse of lawns, punctuated here and there by a gnarled oak in front of the Stuart Rawlings home, where Mrs. Rawlings is frequently visited by her daughter, Mrs. Edward Engs, and several grandchildren.

An old-time creek along the rear of some of the Wildwood lots has long been the central motif around which unusual landscape designs have been created with ferns, rocks and water-cress. The Morton Beebe place is along this intriguing way, and both the house and the generous gardens present ample opportunites for three sons to give many entertainments. Another home nestled beside this creek is that belonging to Mr. Charles C. Keeney, whose deceased wife was the daughter of the late Mr. and Mrs. William G. Henshaw, a distinctive name rating recognition in the Bay Area, New York and even Europe.

Where Wildwood meets Crocker Avenue, the corner house is owned by Jacqueline Valentine. She is the daughter of the late San Francisco attorney, A. A. Moore, who had numerous East Bay connections. Near the Hampton Avenue corner of Crocker one might pause to gaze upon the gentle slope where a large formal mansion was constructed in 1914. Mr. A. A. Moore, Jr., built it for his wife during that year. She had been Florence Blythe before she wed the noted Dr. Hinckley, from whom she was widowed. Together Mr. and Mrs. Moore planned this new estate, enclosing it from prying eyes by high hedges, trees and shrubbery. Their few years of happiness came to an abrupt termination when the husband was killed in a tragic automobile accident. The widow soon departed from the empty house.

But shortly thereafter the dark cloud of sorrow was dissipated when the R. Stanley Dollar family brought to it that spirit of warm hospitality for which they have become justly famous. Diversions were constantly being planned by devoted parents for Stanley and his younger sister Diana. For example, on the grounds of the estate, the Dollars had a glassed-in swimming pool with a luxurious sand beach outside

Craig Home at its present site

and even a life guard in attendance. Diana, with her blonde hair neatly arranged and accompanied by her nurse Marie, could often be seen seated in the light two-seated cart, which was hitched to a stocky Shetland pony. Frequently they would stop by on Craig Avenue to pick up a small friend Ynez and off they would go for a drive.

However, like other parents, the Dollars found the marriage of Diana to Joseph Hickingbotham had removed the *raison d'etre* from life at the big house. This, added to other alterations in family life, caused them to dispose of this estate and follow their inclinations to purchase a more rural home out in the Contra Costa hills. So once again a subdivision has come upon the market, and more families can enjoy life in this setting.

Early Families along Hampton Road . . .

One estate, similar to that of the Dollars and directly across Crocker Avenue, still remains almost untouched in its beauty and undisturbed by any change of ownership. Mrs. Frank Hunt Proctor and her late husband were early residents in that section of the new City. She was merely carrying on a family tradition, as her parents had pioneered the oak-dotted town below. The McDermott Block, covering Seventh, Eighth and Peralta Streets, rated as one of the most elegant and extensive estates to be created in that West Oakland district of wealth and fashion. The daughter, Miss Flora McDermott, was very popular among the youthful social sets who attended the exclusive Deux Tempe dances, and her prestige in Piedmont has remained constant.

Yet another name to be noted among those early comers to the Hampton Road contingent was that of Mr. A. H. Breed, who is known throughout a broad area of California for his activities in politics and real estate. He also served as President of the California State Automobile Association. Under his successful leadership it has grown to wield a tremendous influence toward making touring more pleasurable and safer for an ever increasing number of drivers. He died in April, 1953.

A third family, long established in commercial pursuits in Oakland, became pioneer homemakers on Hampton Road: the senior Mr. and Mrs. Jackson of the furniture business world. Their sons all have since married and are living in Piedmont with their separate families.

Mr. and Mrs. Stuart Hawley lived for many years in one of the finest houses in this neighborhood. But when the son and daughter left to make homes of their own and the husband died, the lonely widow cared no longer to remain. So others have now taken over the beautiful place. Its builders and first occupants were Mr. and Mrs. Gilman from Los Angeles, who lived here with their son and daughter and entertained frequently in the gardens.

Titus and Tyson Tracts ...

Having located in previous pages the names of Titus and Tyson up in a corner of the City maps, that section seems an ideal place to alight for another ramble around the winding circle and on over to St. James Wood.

Perhaps no single avenue in our city of erratic streets has inscribed upon its mailboxes more notable names than are to be found along or in the vicinity of Sotello Avenue. The casual viewer glimpses through trees and shrubbery homes of diverse architectural design. As we begin our walk, we might pass the attractive Fritz Henshaw gardens, and on the curve across the road the William Cavalier home is in plain sight. To the right, as we amble up the drive, are the Lee Tildens in their large white Colonial house, built by the late United States Representative Frank Buck. Mrs. Tilden often opens the spacious rooms for Children's Hospital benefits and her own gay family gatherings.

Mr. and Mrs. R. C. Force lived formerly in the French Provincial house on the high knoll, where the James Tysons had originally hoped to build. The Ward Dawsons, now living on Hillside Avenue, erected a home on that wonderful site, later selling it to the Forces. Continuing around the curves into the Glen Alpine Road, we come across the Jean Witters home, high above its terraced bank. A gold star gleams within this house, keeping bright the memory of the young ensign, Jean Witters, Jr., who with other brave lads was on the *U.S.S. San Francisco* during the battle for the Savo Islands, November, 1942.

Adjacent to the Witters are the Herbert Erskines in a similar setting of superb views. Across the street the Griffith Henshaw house is nestled among trees and shrubbery, as is the home of the Harry H. Fair family. Mrs. Fair is the daughter of the late Mr. and Mrs. Mhoon.

As we turn briskly into Guilford Road, we arrive at the residence of United States Senator William F. Knowland, or such it becomes when his services are not required at the Capitol City. We are indeed proud of the prestige his presence gives to our unique little town.

Descending from that sweeping roadway is the site of the former Ransom-Bridges girls' school.

Return to Highland Avenue ...

Out where Highland Avenue intersects with Hazel Lane, we discover a replica of an English country manor house, constructed in the early twenties by Chaffee Earl Hall, son of the late and distinguished Judge Samuel P. Hall. Mrs. Chaffee Hall came from Alameda as Emmie Lemke, and her innumerable family connections still center about the Bay region.

Off Hazel Lane was carved the new Requa Road through that former twenty acre estate and has given ample opportunity for many diverse and beautiful homes to be built on the large lots. Sufficient proof that this section is holding its own as a top location is given when one glances at the name-plates on each mail box. Perhaps the most generous footage was that acquired by one of the earliest purchasers, Mrs. Crescent Porter Hale. Another of the first places to be developed links together the familiar names of David Brown (famous Stanford runner) and Elizabeth Eby, whose three sons have loftily upheld the family record.

Leaving behind us those gilded gates where centered the social life of a past era, we find the warm pulse of the City spreading to the new and fashionable Sea View Avenue, which stretches north and South across the Crocker tract. Here is portrayed in vibrant colors the picture of the breath of prosperity that swept across the country during the hectic 1920's. Those who built their homes upon the artery comprise a roster of names representative of culture and business, on the San Francisco side as well as upon the Oakland side of the Bay.

Brilliant Names on Sea View Avenue ...

Starting at the northern end of Sea View, one would commence this portion of the ramble at the Harry Knowles house which, to be absolutely accurate, faces on Mountain Avenue, as does Mrs. Mhoon's place close by. On the east side of Sea View is the large bungalow built by Chris Jorgensen, the artist, and his wife, the former Angela Ghirardelli. Moving on along Sea View we see the fine house that was built on the southwest corner by Robert J. Tyson during the first years of the municipal regime. The occupancy by Mr. and Mrs. Tyson was of limited duration, and when its vacancy was announced, the property bas bought by Mrs. William Scott Goodfellow, the widow of a prominent San Francisco attorney. For many years this gracious lady presided over the household and enjoyed occasional visits from her daughters, Mrs. Leon de Fremery and Mrs. Donald Rheem, who lived in the vicinity.

Then the Parisian *maison,* sometimes called the Little Fairmont, of the Edson F. Adams lent a decided style to the Avenue. Mr. and Mrs. Adams celebrated their Golden Wedding Anniversary in 1945 with a formal reception. During the years when Piedmonters would vie with each other over their fabulous decorations of their outdoor trees at Christmas time, this Little Fairmont quietly stole every honorary distinction. Through the glass front doors visitors could gaze directly towards the wide picture-windows looking westward, in front of which stood a tall, star-tipped tree, shimmering in the tinselled glow. In the distant background across the lowlands and stretching across the Bay one could see the shining street-lights surmounting the hills of San Francisco. But after the death of her husband in August, 1946, Mrs. Adams sold her property and moved to smaller quarters in San Francisco.

More Illustrious Citizens . . .

At the date of ownership change Piedmont proudly added to its galaxy of famous names that of the Honorable Joseph R. Knowland, publisher of the *Oakland Tribune* and a gentleman known throughout the State for his contributions to and interest in pioneer and historical societies. Mr. Knowland's parents were early settlers in Alameda in those days when horse-drawn vehicles manuevered across the Estuary through deep muddy ruts or billowing clouds of dust, according to the season. In this present elegant Piedmont home Mr. and Mrs. Knowland entertain guests from far and near with added festivities for their children and grandchildren.

Over on the Lincoln Avenue corner were the Philip Clays in their large Colonial home, built in 1920. From the big rooms radiated a happy family life which was frequently intermixed with charitable and social functions. But in time the son and daughter left, leaving Philip and Edna to take up residence in the Claremont Hotel. Mr. and Mrs. Hendricks became the next owners of this fine home.

Another design of outstanding merit is the huge slate-grey house built for the Gerald Traynors. Albert Farr is once again listed as the architect, and this is a superb example of his mastery of the art. The new owners are Mr. and Mrs. Elgin Stoddard. The wife is known to many Oaklanders and Ebell members as the talented Minna Mc-Gauley.

Continuing along this west side, one comes upon a semi-circular driveway which leads up to the broad front entrance of the Hills Mansion. The three daughters, whose father made Hills Brothers Coffee a famous trademark, have all married and moved elsewhere, but in their day they kept the halls ringing with life and laughter. Orchid culture in the garden below afforded Mrs. Hills (now Mrs. Ellis) a fascinating interest and hobby.

Next comes the Archibald Andrews menage, always with an open door and cheerful welcome for young people who gathered around the parents and sons and daughters. One is glad to know that this household, at least, still keeps its anchorage and traditions firm. While not retaining their old street number, the Andrews are very close by in a lovely, rambling, one floor house, designed and built on a gorgeous lot. They have given it a real Hawaiian touch by the artistic use of native shrubbery in and about the patio, where Mr. and Mrs. Andrews can now enjoy an easier life.

Original Owners Almost Forgotten ...

A well-built house in a lovely setting can proudly fulfill the destiny over several generations of time. Thus it was not long before the old Andrew home took the interest of Mr. and Mrs. Arthur Oppenheimer, Jr. (Phyllis Greenlee). It presented the ideal location for the rearing of their three little sons. Decorators and landscape gardeners gave it a New Look, as young voices once again re-echoed within its walls.

The adjoining property of the late Mrs. Moffitt has now been divided and on one portion now reside Mrs. Catlin and Miss Catlin, who have given to the western suburb an authentic touch of New England culture. Across the Avenue is the estate of Mr. James K. Moffitt, who has already figured in this story. It possesses a particular place in these annals as a center of long established ideals of family tradition.

Several owners of neighboring estates have almost forgotten the original builders. The Moller sisters with their parents were at one time such an acquisition to Piedmont, in their well-designed, plain brick home with its neat green lawns in the foreground. These young ladies belonged to the Delger family of early Oakland, and their native city finally called them back to active service in the various charitable and cultural enterprises to which they belonged. Of their eldest sister this piece was quoted from *A Profile*: "California i rightly proud of its most famous woman engineer, Lillian Moller Gilbreth, U. C., 1900, who has a wonderful capacity for living as well as a genius for scientific management and efficiency."

Next we note the familiar name of Mrs. Eugene K. Sturgis on a name-plate and recall her untiring effort during the formative years before the Women's Athletic Club became a reality. We come then to the Alexander estates of both mother and son, with green spaces of sloping lawns delighting the passing visitors who often claimed that they were viewing a smaller edition of the once-famous Orange Grove Avenue in Pasadena.

Early Pioneers Represented . . .

Crossing the street over to Hampton Road, though still keeping along the main artery of upper Piedmont, on the west corner a high hedge indicates a lengthy period of undisturbed growth. Inside the gateway stands a house more mellowed by the passage of years than most of its neighbors. Walter Starr and his wife (Carmen Moore) were among the first to build upon these country fields. Both came from families who had pioneered about the Bay region a generation earlier: the Moores in East Oakland and the Starrs down Linden Street way. This couple have given their time and effort in the advancement of town affairs. Moreover, Mr. Starr served on the Council for many years after his election in 1914 to the new governing board.

Once again we turn up Glen Alpine Road, where we find the Don Kessler home, well screened from view by a thick hedge. Another large house glimpsed beyond the trees, was built during the upswing of prosperity by Mrs. Williams and her three sons, but this has been sold to others, who, like many more, may be included in later annals of this town.

Before again reaching Sotello, we see the huge Sweetland mansion looming ahead, with its high gables of English architecture, green lawns, rare shrubs and spreading oaks, all making a landscape of exquisite beauty. Mr. and Mrs. Sweetland presented this estate as a rest home to the Catholic nuns, the Sisters of the Holy Family, who had formerly purchased the Butters house at Hillside and Vista Avenues.

The Exclusive St. James Wood . . .

Moving along and turning our steps eastward, we approach the gateway pillars at the entrance of St. James Wood, one of Piedmont's latest sections to be developed. This magnificent location, with its numerous winding avenues and its modernistic homes, might well become the center of a later and more inclusive history. An ambitious contractor started the tract off with a house of French architecture, furnishing it in period style. It was purchased shortly thereafter by George E. Gross, a prominent official of Oakland. His wife Ethel is a daughter of the late Stephen T. Gage, an important California railroad man and intimate friend of Leland Stanford. Gradually, other selected homesites have been landscaped and built upon. The Breuner brothers, Louis, Richard and Wallace, have chosen to live in this neighborhood, each respective home having its garden well equipped for outdoor living.

Then there is Lloyd Stevens of Welsh ancestry whose choice fell upon a rugged hillside for his permanent residence. He earned several high degrees from Stanford University, and Piedmont is truly fortunate in possessing men of such acumen as possible leaders in community advancement.

Continuing up into higher ground where the views are positively breath-taking in their splendor, we come upon a magnificent mansion built on the hillside but with a level approach. Until quite recently it had been the home of Mrs. Richard Ham and her two sons. While the house was yet in the process of construction, a superb concert organ was installed on the lower floor, and it became a central motive for the many Children's Hospital benefits which were often held in the spacious rooms above. The present hostess, Mrs. Archibald, has moved over to Marin County but her generosity and leadership in Community Chest and Red Cross drives has endeared her to a host of friends.

Development of Indian Gulch . . .

Hastening our steps out of St. James Wood into Indian Road, we observe a site of unusual interest situated on an irregular and broken area. Almost hidden by trees with only the entrance visible, the home stands above a canyon where we children of the eighties gathered the wild maiden hair fern and knew that fascinating playground simply as Indian Gulch. This natural beauty spot was selected and improved by the Markwart family and now is the source of much joy for Mrs. Markwart and numerous grandchildren.

Another estate of acreage proportion occupying the corner of Indian Road and La Salle Avenue belonged to Mrs. Wigginton Creed and her daughters. This property, too, has followed the pattern of decrease

holdings. In the gardens where fruit trees, berry vines and table vegetables once flourished, now are to be seen several new homes of modern design.

The Approach of Twilight ...

Retracing our steps, we now make a new start high upon Bellevue Avenue where live Mr. and Mrs. Ehman in their view home, set in its formal gardens. This good couple have given generously of their time and money in fostering worthy causes, especially where music and musicians are concerned. The now popular Oakland Symphony Orchestra, now under the baton of Orley See, is really their dream grown to vivid reality.

Walking towards Mountain Avenue, we approach a wide, sweeping embankment with lawns and trees climbing up to the pretty home built years ago by Katherine Maxwell Bryan and her husband Carlton. The Maxwells are pioneer Oaklanders whose forebears established the hardware store bearing that name.

An adjoining notable home with a driveway opening into Mountain Avenue is that of Dr. Lewis D. Gootschall, the beloved canon of a local Episcopal Church. This house was originally built and occupied by the Mark L. Requa family. Quickening our pace, past the Wing estate where the old home is razed to the ground, we find the spacious house of the active Mrs. Warner Sherwood, whose open doors always gave warm welcome to her daughters' families and friends.

On the Sharon side of the street stands a residence implanted amidst a lively blanket of flowers. Since the early twenties it has been the center of the large and happy Nelson family. The "bit of England" immediately adjacent to this was built about 1904 by the Herbert Hamilton Browns (Florence Sharon).

Soon thereafter we come to the Thayer house, constructed high on the bank overlooking the road; the name Thayer has long been identified with shipping and lumber interests in San Francisco and about the Bay region. Mr. I. E. Thayer came to California in 1862, after a brief service in the Union Army under President Lincoln's first call for volunteers. His active business career commenced shortly thereafter. Records show that in 1868 he presented Mr. Huntington with a laurel tie cut from Mount Tamalpais. It was into this tie that the final golden spike was driven at Promontory Point, Great Salt Lake; this united the Central Pacific and Union Pacific Railroads, thus completing the first transcontinental railroad. At that time Mr. Thayer was a dealer in hardwood timbers used extensively for ship construction.

During 1873 "Captain" Thayer, as his associates called him, brought a young wife from Massachusetts to reside in San Francisco. A little later they moved to Oakland with their son Philip. When the Sharon frontage was placed on the market, they purchased a lot on Mountain Avenue, facing west and commanding a fine view. The residence was erected in 1915, and it has been continuously occupied by the family ever since.

The Pattiani Residence . . .

Over again to the opposite side of the Avenue stands a shingled home more mellowed by the years than its neighbors. It was originally built in 1907 by my husband and myself, but the years spent there were few, as the complete breakdown in his health necessitated the removal of the family to the Napa Valley, where we lived several years for his full recuperation. When we left, the house was taken over by the well known old-time family, the late William Kempkeys, and is now occupied by their daughter, Mrs. Henderson and her youngsters.

On the corner of Dormidera is another of the older homes, which has been owned for a good many years by Mrs. Claire Brayton. Both her own name as one of the "beautiful Tucker sisters", as well as that of her late husband belong to pioneer families with aristocratic backgrounds. Next door on the corner of Pacific Avenue is a house which a snapshot taken in 1922 shows standing in solitary grandeur upon its sunny slope. Mr. and Mrs. Frank Avery were the builders and remained there until they moved up to Sotelo into a more pretentious domicile. Since then they have found a smaller place more to their taste and are at present in an attractive cottage on Indian Road.

King Avenue Revisited . . .

We move again to King Avenue and pass the Dr. McIvor home. The voters selected Mrs. McIvor to serve them upon the Board of Education, and she proved a most efficient worker. She belongs to an early Oakland family, the daughter of Dr. and Mrs. Charles Rowe. Turning off towards the west on to Farragut Avenue, we meet Mrs. William A. Barbour surrounded by her spacious home and garden. She is one of the few remaining members of the Card Club, formed years ago among the Lake District contingent of friends. A daughter, Mrs. Lindberg, and her family are also living in Piedmont.

At the Crocker Avenue corner stands a house built during the early years of settlement of the section by architect Julia Morgan. To it came Ben and Carmen Reed, with their infant son and daughter, thus bringing more descendants of Dominico Chirardelli into Piedmont; for Carmen's mother, Mrs. Sutton, was his eldest daughter. Benjamin Reed also, belonged to an early Alice Street family, and his father still remembered as constructor and owner of Reed Hall at Thirteenth and Harrison Streets, in the days when fashionable dancing clubs were all the craze.

On Farragut Avenue was also located the Walton N. Moore home, where the parents, along with son Joseph and daughter Elizabeth, did much lavish entertaining. The neighboring de Vaux estate also was of this period of unwonted prosperity, but in later years it has been owned by the kindly C. R. Adams.

Final, Slow, Satisfying Stroll ...

On another corner of this intersection lived for many years the popular Charles Bates family. However, the passage of a generation has wrought changes upon them, and now Mrs. Bates (Lucretia Burnam) resides on Hillside Avenue. Now, swiftly glancing over the last two blocks of Sea View, we find the familiar name of Mrs. A. F. Edwards. Many of us can remember that "mark of distinction and quality" on the boxes and bags in which their store delivered gifts and wedding silver.

A home featuring Spanish architecture shelters a family on this Avenue dating back to the days when a pioneer of sterling character, Ezra Decoto, established the town of Decoto in the southern part of Alameda County. The sons who have settled in the northern part have done honor to the name of their forebear. The L. A. Decoto family have found here an ideal location for their home and peaceful living.

So also have others whose names some day will add luster to the rolls of this unique City, located entirely within the confines of the greater City of Oakland.

Travelers from around the world and from high places in government are frequently entertained in these various hospitable homes, and through the broad plate-glass windows they can gaze across San

Francisco Bay and out the Golden Gate, while envisioning beyond the vast stretches of the Pacific and the Far East, where lie problems for future generations to solve.

The wealth of beautiful homes, the extraordinary setting and the general gifts of Nature have given to our Queen City an enviable position throughout the United States. Before it lie opportunities for greater fame as a town of ideal family life, away from the turmoil of crowded centers, nestling among the quiet beauty of the COSY, SUN-LIT HILLS OF PIEDMONT.

APPENDIX I

These social districts included the following:

The Adeline Street neighborhood with its oak-lined avenues—

Adams, Alexanders, Boalt, Chickering, DeFremery, Everson, Hayes, MacDonald, McKee, McNear, Mhoon, Oliver, Prather, Touchard, Whitney, Garber and others.

Then the Market Street contingent came next—

Barker, Drumm, Foote, Hart, Hussey, Coleman, Gray, Nicholson, Sessions, Smith, Starr, Tucker and Wall.

Rivaling this west section were the Jackson Street set—

Brayton, Brown and Brigham, Allen, Chabot, Dyer, Dunham, Clement, Folger, Glascock, Greene, Hamilton, Howard, Houghton, Kirkham, Knowles, Hubbard, Latham, Lohman, Metcalf, Ralston, Shafter, Stanford, Steele, Soule, Upham, Watt, Wheaton, Wadsworth, Wilson and Gordon.

From outlying districts came these—

Ainsworth, Bray, Campbell, Deans, Eells, Gamble, Grimes, Hunt, Livermore, Requa, Sheppard, Pierce, Tevis and Trebbs, and Watkinson.

Not all, but many of these foregoing names were later inscribed upon Piedmont records as landholders.

APPENDIX II

From Fruitvale Avenue and East Fourteenth Street came the Henry Wetherbees and the Wellmans.

In that same vicinity could be found the homes of A. W. Bray, Judge Crockett, A. M. Derby, Grimwood, J. West Martin, Mr. Requa, brother of Isaac L. Requa, and Joshua Tevis.

Further along the Fruitvale Avenue section were the Clays, Duncans, Judge Warner Earll, the Hinckleys and Stevensons.

APPENDIX III

Among a few names recalled are those of Moffitt, Clay, Adams, Havens, Johnson, Alexander, Chickering, Moore, Starr, Stanford, Playter and Potter. These families, along with other arrivals during succeeding years, have given a distinctive prestige to Piedmont. Rated among the population are presidents and executives of business firms with extensive interests throughout the Western States. In the Sixth Period their achievements are mentioned.

APPENDIX IV

From the *Piedmont News,* May 27, 1921:

"Mrs. James K. Moffitt gave a tea at her home, having as her guest of honor Mrs. A. A. Moore, whose marriage to Dr. William Musgrave will take place in the fall. Mrs. Moffitt had as her guests Mesdames Wallace M. Alexander, Donald McClure, Walter Starr, Mark Lawrence Requa, John J. Valentine, Leon Bocqueraz, Florence Sharon Brown, John Deickmann, Stuart Rawlings, William A. Magee, Frank Stringham, John Bell Mhoon, Stanley Moore, Oscar Sutro, James P. H. Dunne; Misses Jane Rawlings, Annie Miller and others."

APPENDIX V

The members of the original Board of Education in Piedmont were Adolph Uhl, Fred Sercombe and Charles Hill. Piedmont became an "A" school district, July 1, 1926, and then a unified school district, July, 1936. The schools making up the system are as follows:

Havens School	Built 1908-1909	
	Addition completed	August 26, 1936
Beach School	Built	1913
	Addition completed	November, 1936
High School	Built	July 27, 1921
	Addition completed	December, 1935
Junior High School	Built	June, 1924
Wildwood School	Opened	August 26, 1936

APPENDIX VI

Officers of the Piedmont Musical Club:

Mrs. H. Melville Tenney, President
Mr. Samuel H. Taylor, Vice-President
Mr. W. D. Tillinghast, Treasurer
Mrs. W. H. Wakefield, Corresponding Secretary
Mr. George W. Banzhaf, Recording Secretary
Mrs. Murray L. Johnson, Hospitality Chairman

Committee members were Luella Wagor Coplin, Lena Carroll Nicholson, Mr. and Mrs. Orley See and Esta Pomeroy.

APPENDIX VII

Those present at the first meeting of the Piedmont Men's Club were the following: Messrs. J. E. Stuchell, Mark L. Requa, Waldron,

W. V. Dinsmore, Charles T. Bliss, L. Norris, Roeth, Herbert H. Brown, Oscar Sutro, Searless, A. J. Pillsbury, Redmond, Robertson, H. Farr, Robert Tyson, Jackson, Jason and Dr. Brinckerhoff.

APPENDIX VIII

A few of the members of the Red Cross League were Mrs. Wallace Alexander, Mesdames Walter Starr, Ethel Bates Lee, Santilier, Lillie Downie, Oliver Haslett, Stuart Rawlings, Maude Allen, Kergan and Gisela Haslett.

BOOKS USED AS REFERENCES

Adams, Edson F.: *History of Early Oakland.*
Bailey, Millard: *History of San Francisco Bay Region.*
Baker, James E.: *History of Alameda County, (1914).*
———: *Past and Present in Alameda County.*
Cleland, Robert Glass: *Wilderness to Empire: an Economic History of California in Our Time.*
Elliott, W. W.: *Oakland and Surroundings* (Oakland, California: 1884).
Halley, William: *History of Alameda County* (1876).
Hittel, John S.: *History of San Francisco* (1878).
Hittel, Theodore: *History of California.*
Ives, S. N.: *Altadena* (1938).
Kahn, Edward M.: *Cable Car Days.*
Merritt, F. C.: *History of Alameda County.*
O'Sullivan, Mrs. Denis: *Harry Butters, RFA, An American Citizen.*
Shutes, Dr. Milton: *Abraham Lincoln.*
From the Key System Transit Company Library:
Economic History of Transportation in the East Bay: Vol. I, by Dallas W. Smythe.